WRITERS AND THEIR WORK

ISOBEL ARMSTRONG
Consultant Editor

BEN OKRI

BEN OKRI:

TOWARDS THE INVISIBLE CITY

Robert Fraser

© Copyright 2002 and 2013 by Robert Fraser, 1947–

First published in 2002 by Northcote House Publishers Ltd, Horndon, Tavistock, Devon, PL19 9NQ, United Kingdom.
Tel: +44 (01822) 810066. Fax: +44 (01822) 810034.
www.writersandtheirwork.co.uk

Reprinted with additions 2013

British Library Cataloguing-in-Publication Data
A catalogue record for this book is available from the British Library

ISBN 978-0-7463-0993-3

Typeset by TW Typesetting, Plymouth, Devon

Printed and bound by CPI Group (UK) Ltd, Croydon, CR0 4YY

For Sandra Ponzanesi
una sublime mente

ALSO BY ROBERT FRASER:

Proust and the Victorians: The Lamp of Memory

The Making of The Golden Bough: *The Origins and Growth of An Argument*

Edward Brathwaite's Masks

Lifting the Sentence: A Poetics of Postcolonial Fiction

The Novels of Ayi Kwei Armah: A Study in Polemical Fiction

West African Poetry: A Critical History

Victorian Quest Romance: Stevenson, Haggard, Kipling and Conan Doyle

The Chameleon Poet: A Life of George Barker

Book History Through Postcolonial Eyes: Re-writing the Script

Night Thoughts: The Surreal Life of the Poet David Gascoyne

AS EDITOR:

The Collected Poems of George Barker

The Selected Poems of George Barker

Reading African Poetry

This Island Place

Sir James Frazer and the Literary Imagination: Essays in Affinity and Influence

The Golden Bough: A New Abridgement

FOR THE THEATRE:

God's Good Englishman

Gesualdo

"Very Naughty O ...": Lord Byron's Italian Love Affair

Something in the Air

Contents

Preface

To begin with I offer a few visible – and hence possibly insignificant – facts. I have been reading and reviewing the work of Ben Okri for thirty years, and have known him for slightly longer. We first met over Sunday lunch at a house in Greenwich, south London, on 14 December 1980. Our hostess, from whose carefully kept diary this detail comes, was the social activist and Bessie Head scholar, Jane Grant. Head herself was there, stocky and indomitable as ever, chain-smoking over the food. That summer Okri had published his novel *Flowers and Shadows*, and a few months earlier I had brought out my first, short monograph: a study of the Ghanaian novelist Ayi Kwei Armah. To my eternal shame, Ben had read my book, but I had not then read his.

I cannot recall anything that we said to one another on this occasion, but we soon fell into a friendship that, on both our parts, possessed an element of reciprocal self-mockery. My impression of that time is that Ben always wore a red beret. (Probably he wore it only once or twice, but it is the essence of what the French critic Gérard Genette once called the 'pseudo-iterative' tense that isolated occasions expand in the memory into continuities.) During the ensuing months the downstairs bar at the Africa Centre in King Street, Covent Garden, became our meeting place, sometimes our stomping ground. I still possess a grainy photographic print of Ben – in his red beret naturally – reading his poems aloud in the ground floor auditorium. It was taken on Saturday, 26 March 1983, during one of the annual poetry-and-music events organized each spring by a generous and literature-obsessed psychotherapist, Dr Pat Gillan. In that smoke-filled, enthusiastic space we each performed our work to the rambling accompaniment of James Danton's jazz band. A mutual acquaintance of ours, now a career diplomat, once told me that he had observed us afterwards pirouetting in ballet formation with umbrellas in the open street on our way to the post-reading bash in Tilson Gardens, SW2. His reminiscence is, I am sure, pure make-believe, but it does convey something of the pedantic caprice, the grave but farcical *folie de grandeur*, in which we then both delighted

Jokes were an important ingredient of this relationship, but they did not constitute its essence. The heart of it – as of Ben himself – was a deep, protected seriousness. Even in those early days, there was something about Okri that was evident to everyone: a single-minded dedication to writing fiction, from which he would allow little to distract him. Many people in their earlier twenties seem inexplicably confused as to how to spend the rest of their lives. Ben in stark contrast showed, and I am sure experienced, no uncertainty whatsoever. He lived to write books and to read them, two activities so complementary as to amount almost to the same devotion. There were to be many opportunities along the way for him to abscond into a range of subordinate worlds or activities: journalism, broadcasting, humanitarian commitment, the lecturing circuit. Each of these was to claim its place in his life (especially, as will become clear, humanitarian concern). In the larger scheme of things, however, they represented – to quote his personal and universal allegory of 1995, *Astonishing the Gods* – 'negative dreams that test and tempt those who might receive prizes from the Academy of Integrity'. In practice, therefore, none was to mean much except as a means of amplifying the resources of the centred – and centring – imagination.

Time went by, and we both grew a bit more solemn, at least on the surface. We succeeded one another in the same job: the poetry editorship of the London-based weekly *West Africa*, a position created in 1978 by its then editor Kenneth McKenzie and offered, following my resignation in 1983, to Ben. (There had been no need to resign; I should, as I realized later, simply have asked for a rise.) Eight years later we became colleagues at the largest and most affluent college in Cambridge, a development that in the early 1980s we would have considered so unlikely as to pertain to the universe of *Alice in Wonderland* (in certain respects, it did so.) These were eventful years. On Tuesday, 22 October 1991, a fortnight after arriving in Cambridge, Ben won the Booker McConnell Prize for Fiction, the picked cherry amongst literary awards, for his third novel, *The Famished Road*; I meanwhile was busy preparing a study of Proust. We returned to London, though to different banks of the Thames. There were publishers' launches for successive books, birthday parties each March at the Ivy. For my own fiftieth birthday party he arrived in darkest south London by taxi bearing a clutch of contrasted presents: a black 'Chester' style trilby hat; Gillon R. Aitken's translation of *The Complete Prose Tales of Alexandr Sergeyevitch Pushkin*; and Amir D. Aczel's mathematical thriller, *Fermat's Last Theorem*. Flamboyance; intellectual adventure; austerity: all lay implicit within that treble choice.

Under the circumstances it has been difficult at moments to prevent this essay assuming the aspect of a memoir. My principal focus throughout, however, is on Okri's work. What I have tried to do is to dovetail a few background details from his life with the essential facts of recent Nigerian history, creating a trellis around which I have draped a discussion of his contributions as writer of fiction, essayist, social activist, and poet. The result is, amongst other things, an essay on the place of the writer in the contemporary world. Not of any author, but of a particular kind of artist, one who in vital respects resists the mainstream. Ben Okri does not fit comfortably into any of the received critical categories. To the extent that his work rebels against this climate of opinion, it interrogates the prevailing discourses of our time. In what follows, the consequences of such exceptionality constitute a secondary, but still salient, theme.

Robert Fraser

Acknowledgements

I have discussed the art of African fiction over the years with very many people, including Buchi Emecheta, Drs Ato Quayson and Alastair Niven, Ama Ata Aidoo, Professors Gerald Moore and Dennis Walder, and the late Dambudzo Marechera. In their various ways all of these people have sharpened my reading. For matters of background I am indebted to the playwright Oladipo Agboluaje and that literary genius of all trades, Biyi Bandele. For specific pieces of information, I wish to thank Zoe Fairbairns, Jane Grant, Dr James Gibbs, Dr Andrew Nicholson, the Revd Dr Arnold Browne, and Professors Lyn Innes and Francesca Butari. On relevant philosophical subjects I have been guided by Dr Nick Denyer (who, furthermore, once provided me with incontrovertible proof for the existence of God, set out in logical symbolism. I failed to understand – and then lost – it). Since 1980 I have also enjoyed numerous intellectual explorations with Ben Okri himself, both recorded and unrecorded. His only piece of advice to me whilst engaged on this book, however, was 'For God's sake, don't turn me into a *post*-anything', an exhortation that I have followed to the letter. In all other respects, I alone am responsible for the views on his work across a variety of *genres* expressed in these pages. The same goes for my interpretations of West African history, and of a continuing – and volatile – Nigerian situation. The book's shortcomings are all my own.

Biographical Outline

1959   On Sunday, 15 March, Ben Okri is born in the railway town of Minna in central Nigeria, one of four children – three sons and a daughter – of Silver Oghenegueke Loloje Okri, an Urhobo from near Warri on the Niger delta, and his wife, Grace, an Igbo from the Mid-West.

1960   On 1 October, Nigeria attains its independence from the United Kingdom to become a nation state under a federal constitution, but with a northern-dominated parliament. To celebrate the fact of independence, Wole Soyinka's epic drama *A Dance of the Forests* is performed in the (then) capital city of Lagos and in the university town of Ibadan.

1961   Silver Okri journeys to London, where he reads for the bar examinations at the Inner Temple. After the family has joined him, the Okris settle in Peckham in the Borough of Southwark, where from September 1964 Ben attends John Donne Primary School on Woods Road.

1963   In August the Mid-Western Region of Nigeria is created. Symptoms of strain in the federation appear in September as Chief Obafemi Awolowo, first premier of the Western Region, is imprisoned on charges of attempting to undermine the national leadership. In October the country becomes a republic.

1965   In July, Silver Okri is called to the British bar. The family return to Nigeria, where Ben continues his primary education at the Children's Home School in Sapele, fifty miles to the north of Warri. Publication of Soyinka's novel *The Interpreters*.

1966   Civilian administration in Nigeria comes to an abrupt end with two successive military *coups d'état*. In the first, on 15 January, the federal Prime Minister, Sir Abukakar Tafawa Balewa, is assassinated by a cabal of junior army officers. In February, an attempt to set up an independent state in the delta region is suppressed after twelve days. After assuming leadership of the military government, Major-General Johnson Aguiyi-Ironsi, an Igbo, decrees a unitary administration for the whole country. Silver Okri is enrolled in the Nigerian bar on Friday, 22 July. A week later, on Friday, 29 July, Aguiyi-Aronsi is murdered in a second *coup*, to be replaced by Lieutenant-General (later General) Yakubu Gowon. In October, pogroms in the Northern – Hausa-dominated – city of Kano, result in the massacre of several thousand Igbos, migrant workers from the economically advantaged east.

1967　In January the Aburi conference in Ghana, held on the Akwapim heights overlooking Accra, reaches an accord that Gowon decides not to implement. On 27 May he announces a new division of the country into twelve states. Three days later Lieutenant-Colonel (later General) Odumegwu Ojukwu announces the secession of the three easternmost states as the autonomous Republic of Biafra. Christopher Okigbo, Nigeria's most accomplished poet, resigns as representative for the Cambridge University Press in Ibadan to join the Biafran army as a major. In August, he dies at the Battle of Nsukka. Advancing westwards, the Biafrans temporarily capture Warri. Soyinka is arrested by the federal authorities for attempting to form a Third Force to oppose the war. For two years, two months, he is held in prisons at Ibadan, Lagos, and Kaduna; he will later recount these experiences in an acerbic memoir, *The Man Died* (1972). Ben attends Christ's High School at Ibadan in the Western State.

1970　Biafra is gradually reduced to a shrinking enclave. On 15 January, a Biafran delegation surrenders in Lagos. From September, Ben attends secondary school as a boarder at Urhobo College, Warri.

1975　After postponing the 1974 deadline for a return to civilian rule, Gowon is ousted on 25 January by Briga-

xvi

dier Murtala Ramat Mohammed, who is himself assassinated on 13 February and replaced by Lieutenant-General Olusegun Obasanjo. Leaving Urhobo College, Ben studies privately in Lagos, experimenting with both writing and painting. Deciding that his primary talent is for writing, he starts work on his first novel, *Flowers and Shadows*, set in Lagos and completed in manuscript by his nineteenth birthday. Whilst preparing to read science at university, he works in the commercial division of ICI, valuable experience for the economic background to the book. Nigeria's twelve states are further subdivided into nineteen.

1978   After failing to find a place on a local science degree course, Okri travels to London, taking the manuscript of *Flowers and Shadows* with him. He lives with his uncle in New Cross, then in a bedsit in Plumstead, whilst working as staff writer and librarian for the France-based current affairs digest *Afroscope*, and attending evening classes in Afro-Caribbean literature at Goldsmiths College.

1979   On 1 October, Shehu Usman Aliju Shagari, a Northerner, is elected President of the Second Republic. *Flowers and Shadows* is accepted by the British firm, Longman, who publish it the following summer in their new 'Drumbeat' Series, launched in 1979 as a showcase for recent African fiction.

1980   Awarded a Nigerian government scholarship, Okri enrols at the University of Essex, reading for a BA in Comparative Literature.

1981   Okri has an unpublished play performed at Essex. His second novel, *The Landscapes Within*, also set in Lagos, is issued by Longman that December.

1982   As a result of the Shagari government's austerity measures, Okri's scholarship is curtailed. He moves back to London, where, after a period of homelessness, he rents a flat in Seven Sisters, later moving to successive apartments in west London.

1983   Shagari is re-elected as President of Nigeria. Okri is appointed Poetry Editor of the weekly magazine *West Africa*, based at Holborn Viaduct, London EC1. He is simultaneously employed freelance by the BBC African Service at Bush House in the Strand to introduce the current affairs and features programme *Network Africa,* appearing opposite the career broadcaster Hilton Fyle. He revisits Nigeria, where, on 31 December, Shagari is overthrown by a *coup* (the country's fifth). Major-General Mohammed Butari now forms a draconian Supreme Military Council, suppressing all democratic rights.

1984   Okri is awarded a bursary by the Arts Council of Great Britain.

1985   On 27 August, Butari is himself overthrown by Major-General Ibrahim Babangida, whose Armed Forces Ruling Council promises a second return to civilian rule by the early 1990s. While visiting Nigeria in November, Okri observes the consequences of the new government's 'War against Indiscipline'. Several of his essays are published in the left-of-centre current affairs weekly the *New Statesman.*

1986   Okri's volume of shorter fictions, *Incidents at the Shrine,* is published by William Heinemann. It is widely and appreciatively reviewed by the mainstream British press, winning the Commonwealth Prize for Fiction and the Paris Review Aga Khan Prize for fiction, both in 1987. From now on, he earns his living as a writer.

1988   A second volume of shorter fiction, *Stars of the Late Curfew,* is published by Secker & Warburg. It is widely reviewed in Britain and America.

1990   In Nigeria's oil-rich but politically suppressed deltas region, MOSOP (The Movement for the Survival of the Ogoni People) is formed as a voice for the Ogoni people living around Port Harcourt and Bonny Island, and to demand compensation from Shell Petroleum for polluting the local environment.

1991   On Monday, 18 March, *The Famished Road,* first novel in a sequence of that name, is launched by Jonathan Cape, whose commissioning editor David Godwin becomes Ben's committed advocate. Initially there are few reviews. On Friday, 19 July, Okri is offered, and accepts, a two-year Fellow Commonorship in Creative Arts at

Trinity College, Cambridge. He takes up the appointment on Tuesday, 8 October. On Tuesday, 22 October, *The Famished Road* wins the Booker McConnell Prize for Fiction. Nigeria is once again subdivided, this time into thirty states.

1992 A volume of poetry, *An African Elegy*, is published by Cape in March. Following the American publication of *The Famished Road* in May, Okri sails on a promotional trip to the USA in July.

1993 In January, Babangida dissolves the AFRC and forms a transitional government consisting of a predominantly military National Defence and Security Council, and a civilian council of ministers. In March, *Songs of Enchantment*, the second volume of 'The Famished Road' sequence, is published by Cape. In June, national elections in Nigeria are annulled by the NDSC. Babangida subsequently resigns amidst political turmoil. In November, yet another military *coup* brings to power a northern military cabal dominated by General Sani Abacha.

1994 On 21 May, nine officials of MOSOP, including its President, the author Ken Saro-Wiwa, are held by the military government without trial.

1995 In February, Saro-Wiwa and his seven detainees are put on trial for treason. Their cause is widely adopted by the international literary community, with Okri active in the protests. In March (former) General Obasanjo and forty-three others are detained for demanding a swift return to civilian rule. The same month, Okri's allegory, *Astonishing the Gods*, is brought out by his new publisher, Phoenix House. The World Economic Forum presents him with its Crystal Award for contributions to the Arts and to cross-cultural understanding. *Birds of Heaven*, a short compilation of his recent speeches and essays, is issued by Phoenix as a 60 pence booklet. On 31 October, Saro-Wiwa and his fellow detainees are sentenced to death by hanging. Despite a personal appeal from President Nelson Mandela of South Africa and candle-lit vigils in London and elsewhere, the sentence is carried out on 10 November.

1996 *Dangerous Love*, Okri's revision of his earlier novel *The Landscapes Within* (1981), is published by Phoenix. For the BBC television series *Great Railway Journeys* he travels via France, Switzerland, Venice, and Brindisi to the Peloponnese in search of a legendary Arcadia where 'the human spirit can be serene'.

1997 *A Way of Being Free*, a longer collation of Okri's speeches, essays, and reviews, is published by Phoenix. He is made Doctor of Letters *honoris causa* by the University of Westminster. He is elected a Vice-President of the English Centre of the writer's association, International PEN.

1998 *Infinite Riches*, the third volume in 'The Famished Road' sequence, is published by Phoenix. Okri is elected Fellow of the Royal Society of Literature. In June, General Abacha dies of a heart attack, reputedly after taking an overdose of the drug Viagra. An interim government takes over under General Abdulsalam Abubakar, pledged to return the country to civilian rule.

1999 Two sections of the Blakean *Mental Fight*, Okri's salute to the millennium, are published in *The Times* in January. The poem in its entirety is issued by Phoenix later in the year. After elections in May, Nigeria begins its third experiment with civilian government as former General Obasanjo is installed as President.

2000 Okri serves as Chairman of the Judges for the Caine Prize for African Fiction, established in memory of the late Sir Michael Caine (1927–99), for twenty-five years Chairman of the Booker Prize management committee. In October, during three days of rioting between Yoruba and Hausa elements in Lagos, 100 fatalities are recorded. In the north, Christian churches are attacked.

2001 Okri is awarded an OBE in the Queen's Birthday Honours List. In October, clashes between Muslim and Christian youths occur in Kano in the wake of American and British air raids over Afghanistan.

2002 Okri's novel *In Arcadia* takes its title from an abbreviation of 'Et in Arcadia ego', a motto found in two paintings by Nicolas Poussin (1594–1665) and quoted by Evelyn Waugh in the Oxford sequence of the nostalgic classic *Brideshead Revisited* (1945). The narrative draws on Okri's train journey to Greece in 1996, and centres on a group of travellers to a country that is part mythical, part mental, part real. As in Poussin, however, the idyllic destination is ambiguous.

2003 Olusegun Obasanjo is re-elected as President of Nigeria.

2007 Publication of Okri's allegorical novel *Starbook*, beginning with the words 'This is a story my mother began to tell me when I was a child. The rest I gleaned from the book of life among the stars, in which all things are known.' What follows is a fable of the complicated responsibilities of literature and art. In June, after a controversial election and amid continuing ethnic strife, Umanu Yar'Adua, a former Governor of Katsina, is elected President of Nigeria at the head of a coalition government.

2010 On Yar'Adua's death on May 5, his Vice-President Dr Goodluck Jonathan succeeds him, to be elected in his own right in 2011. The new election is followed by further violence in the North.

2012 Islamicist militants set up a secessionist government in the North of Mali. In the ancient city of Timbuctoo, several Sufi shrines are destroyed.

2013 French forces intervene to restore order in Mali. By the time the jihadist militants have withdrawn from Timbuctoo, several thousand historic manuscripts written in the ajami script have been destroyed.

Abbreviations

AE	*An African Elegy* (London: Jonathan Cape, 1992)
AG	*Astonishing the Gods* (London: Phoenix House, 1995)
BH	*Birds of Heaven* (London: Phoenix House: 1996)
DL	*Dangerous Love* (London: Phoenix House, 1996)
FR	*The Famished Road* (London: Jonathan Cape, 1991)
FS	*Flowers and Shadows* (Harlow: Longman, 1989)
IR	*Infinite Riches* (London: Phoenix House, 1998)
IS	*Incidents at the Shrine* (London: Heinemann, 1986)
LW	*The Landscapes Within* (Harlow: Longman, 1982)
MF	*Mental Fight* (London: Phoenix House, 1999)
SE	*Songs of Enchantment* (London: Jonathan Cape, 1993)
SNC	*Stars of the New Curfew* (London: Secker and Warburg, 1988)
WBF	*A Way of Being Free* (London: Phoenix House, 1997)

1

A Dance of Descriptions

Names have a way of making things disappear.
(Ben Okri, *Astonishing the Gods*)

Names are like points; propositions like arrows.
(Ludwig Wittgenstein,
Tractatus Logico-Philosophicus)

In 1996 Ben Okri published an essay called 'Beyond Words', based on a sermon delivered three years earlier in the Elizabethan chapel of Trinity College, Cambridge.[1] The essay-cum-address represented a deeply thought-out assessment by a practising author of the means and consequences of his art (*WBF* 88–95). Its subject was the efficacy – and the limitations – of language.

First, Okri declared, words can describe – but they can also misdescribe – reality. When employed to misdescribe, they can prove treacherous, even fatal. Lastly, words can go only so far in the evocation of the world. There are certain tasks for which they seem ideally suited, others for which they are patently not designed. When it enters the latter territory, language must falter, soar into transcendence, or else cease. Sometimes – frequently the most important times – it is best to be silent.

These observations are suggestive for a number of reasons. They pose several of the most ancient – and still most relevant – questions in the philosophy of meaning. They elucidate a number of problems in the modern world, especially in Africa, above all in Okri's Nigeria. They also shed light on the critical reception of Okri's own work. I would like to start by thinking about one particular aspect of Okri's argument: his statements about the potentially destructive effects of language. Words

1

seem well equipped for certain purposes. How is it, then, that this very equipment occasionally proves so harmful?

NOT PERCHING BUT FLYING

The limitations of language that Okri has in mind are of different kinds, one of which has to do with the boundaries between various uses to which words are put. We can illustrate it by invoking a distinction well known to African and European philosophies, a distinction moreover cited by a founding father of modern African fiction and echoed by Okri himself.[2]

In his novel *Things Fall Apart* Chinua Achebe describes how the young hero Okonkwo pays a courtesy call to the hut of an elder called Nwakibie. Nwakibie is deeply impressed by this up-and-coming fellow countryman. He announces to the younger man that he is prepared to invest in his farm by donating 800 yam seeds. This decision, as he carefully explains, represents an act less of generosity than of prudence. The seeds will, he is sure, be put to good use. Nwakibie then quotes an old proverb uttered by a fleet-winged creature called 'Eneke-nti-oba': 'Eneke the bird says that since men have learned to shoot without missing, he has leaned to fly without perching.'[3] To avoid adversity, Nwakibie implies, one needs, like Eneke the bird, to move nimbly.

Anybody who has done the most elementary ornithology, or who has observed hunters at work, will appreciate this Igbo adage. A bird resting on a branch can be so still as to appear lifeless; once on the wing, it is almost too swift for human eye to follow. A stationary bird can be summed up as a whole – visually or verbally – because it is halfway to being a hieroglyph. With a steady aim, it can also be shot with ease. Fully to convey in language the flurry of movements that compose flight, however, would exhaust paragraphs, chapters, volumes of text. To pot a bird on the wing, what is more, is a task for experienced marksmen.

In this respect, bird stalking is much like language. The philosopher Ludwig Wittgenstein once drew an equivalent distinction, which he put like this. There is one verbal operation called 'naming' and another called 'describing'.[4] The first is appropriate to static entities or objects; the second to happenings, narratives, or 'facts'. A semantic confusion arises when you muddle up these categories – for example, by fixing a name to a complex event, a set of assertions, or a sequence of actions. To put the argument in Achebe's terms, naming something is like forcing a bird to perch. Description, by contrast, is like attempting to follow a bird in full flight, a much more demanding task, as difficult in its way as telling a story.

Such distinctions between varieties of perception, and the language associated with them, may seem arcane, yet the implications of failing to observe them can be extreme. The naming of complicated events is always a feat of simplification relying, as Okri says in his sermon-turned-essay, on 'Words that conceal. Words that reduce' (*WBF* 88). As Okri and Wittgenstein are both aware – as the recent histories of Africa, Eastern Europe, and the Middle East have disturbingly taught us – the confusion between labelling and describing, between objects and events, sometimes leads to genocide or war.

THE INVENTION OF LANGUAGE

Okri conveys the force of this observation in his novel *Songs of Enchantment* through a parable told to the spirit child Azaro by his mother (*SE* 73–8). Once, she tells him, human beings lived in accord. Nobody owned anything, and all men and women were omniscient. 'They had no language as such'. Then, out of nowhere, the very first rainbow appeared: 'a young man said, "I saw the rainbow first. It is mine".' It was the first ever spoken statement, and it concerned naming and ownership. The young man's covetousness bred contention; contention provoked violence. People now possessed the tool of language but 'they no longer understood one another. They broke into tribes. They had wars all of the time. And they moved away from the great garden that was their home.'

Losing patience, God sent down Death, who wreaked havoc on earth. Still the quarrelling did not cease. So God dispatched a tiny bird, who immediately turned into a child and went off

3

to confront Death in his lair. The infant informed the grim destroyer that he would cause him to perish in his turn. The destroyer laughed, inquiring with derision, 'How can you kill death?' 'With love,' the child replied (*SE* 76).

This parable combines and reworks three Old Testament motifs: the Flood, the Tower of Babel, and the Fall. In Genesis the first rainbow is a sign by God proclaiming a covenant between himself and humans, potentially between humans as well. In Okri's version, it becomes the original source of contention, before which humans lived in Paradise. In Genesis they were forced to leave the Garden of Eden because they ate of a forbidden fruit, learning in the process about good, evil, and shame. In Okri's alternative creation myth they drift away from perfection because they have learned how to speak, and hence to argue. Language is the harbinger of violence. Most damaging is naming – the kind of language that takes aim and declares 'I name this. This is mine.'

THE BABEL OF NATIONHOOD

In Okri's parable from *Songs of Enchantment* the expulsion from the garden has dire consequences, one of which is specifically identified: the fragmenting of humanity into 'tribes'. The use of this term is itself a clue to a complex and connected historical reality. To trace its reverberations, it may be helpful to look at another episode from one of Okri's later novels.

In *Infinite Riches*, the irrepressible Madame Koto dreams that she is giving birth to a sprawling country: 'an unruly nation, bursting with diversity'. It is a place abounding in all sorts of human potential, but its citizens 'were too many, too different, too contradictory: the nation was composed not of one people but of several mapped and bound in one artificial entity by Empire builders' (*IR* 201–2).

This nation of which Madame Koto dreams bears some resemblance to Nigeria, a country whose cultural roots are inconceivably ancient, but which as a political entity is comparatively recent. The oldest Nigerian civilization known to archaelogists is the Iron Age Nok culture of the Benue plateau, thought to date back to 800BCE, making it almost

4

contemporaneous with the Greek poet Sappho. From that time on, occupation of the Sahelian and forest zones has been continuous. An imperialist myth once prevailed to the effect that the communities occupying this large area had no literature or philosophy. In fact, at least from the time of the Arab incursions into the north around 1000CE, literature flourished there, though the principal means of cultural transmission, especially in the south, remained word or mouth. (In the wider African context, by contrast, the kingdom of Meroe to the far north-east possessed its own script, whilst the culture of Egypt pre-dates the Athens of Pericles by over 1,000 years). When the Scottish explorer Mungo Park visited the Sahelian region twice in the early nineteenth century, he found Koranic schools wherever he went. He even gave a New Testament in Arabic to a local chief in exchange for supplies.[5]

The world beyond Africa has been reluctant to acknowledge these facts, even when they are staring them in the face. To illustrate this blind spot, Okri introduces into *Infinite Riches* a colonial governor on the verge of retirement. A preposterous and prolix man with a polyp on the end of his nose, he is engaged in writing his memoirs. Patronizing in tone, their view of history is shallow:

> The Governor-General, in his re-writing of our history, deprived us of language, of poetry, of stories, of architecture, of civil laws, of social organization, of art, science, mathematics, sculpture, abstract conception, and philosophy. He deprived us of history, of civilization and, unintentionally, of humanity too. Unwittingly, he effaced us from creation. And then, somewhat startled at where his rigorous logic had led him, he performed the dexterous feat of investing us with life the moment his ancestors set eyes on us as we slept through the great roll of historical time. (*IR* 111)

Not content with plundering Africa's material wealth, the Governor, and the colonial order he represents, have scratched out the continent's complicated past with the stroke of a pen.

To be honest, the Governor General of *Infinite Riches* is an unusually thick-witted example of his kind. By and large, the British who took over the mass of local cultures in this part of West Africa, grouping them into a colony they called Nigeria, did acknowledge the prior existence of diverse histories and types of social organization. But they espoused a number of connected misconceptions. First, they, assumed that all these cultural and political units could be fixed and named. Secondly, they took for granted the existence of quasi-permanent hierarchies between and within ethnic groups. Thirdly, they placed an unwise bet on the feasibility of knocking everybody into one coherent colony and, potentially, nation.

Consider the Mid-West, Okri's motherland and fatherland. The coastal area between Port Harcourt in the east and Warri in the west is an extended tableland watered by the contiguous basins of the Niger and Osse rivers. Towards the sea, it peters out into a complicated congeries of creeks; inland, it broadens into the plain around Benin in one direction and, in the other, the country around Lokoja where the Niger and Benue rivers join. No ethnic or language group predominates over this vast area. Instead, there is a complex overlapping of different peoples. In the creeks, the Ijọ rub shoulders with Okri's father's people, the Urhobo, and with his mother's, the Mid-Western Igbo. In the seaport of Warri, where Ben did his secondary schooling, all three groups live in uneasy proximity with the Itsekiri, friction with whom is documented as far back as 1884;[6] it flared up again in 1999.

On arriving at this point along the West African coast in the 1480s, the Europeans – initially the Portuguese – had two declared aims: to siphon off the inland trade, and to reach and conquer the important empire of Benin to the north. They overlooked realities that did not contribute to these grand designs. To achieve the first, they established relations with a number of coastal peoples: the Efik towards the east, and – westwards – the Ijọ and Itsekiri. Groups such as the Urhobo, Ibibio, and inland Igbo without access to the ocean were at first largely ignored. Though the Urhobo had developed valuable skills as harvesters of palm oil and kernels, they enjoyed little contact with the newcomers, and no representation to advance their interests. This anomaly came to a head in 1884, when the British named an Itsekiri aristocrat called Nana Olumu 'Governor' over the entire region, a situation that worsened from the Urhobo point of view in 1897 when another Itsekiri chieftian, Dogho Numa, was named paramount chief of Warri province.[7] This imbalance caused widespread resentment among the Urhobo, who soon founded a 'Brotherly Society', subsequently renamed a 'Progress Union' to further their cause. Despite this, until 1914, the year of the amalgamation of the colonies of Northern and Southern Nigeria, the Urhobo had no primary schools. The first secondary school had to wait until the setting-up of Okri's *alma mater*, Urhobo College, in the late 1940s.

Independence made little immediate difference to this pattern of appropriation and naming. Warri was now part of the Western Region of the country, dominated by the Action Group Party under the Yoruba panjandrum, Obafemi Awolowo. The party further complicated matters by upgrading the title of the Itsekiri paramount chief from 'Olu of Itsekiri' to 'Olu of Warri', implicitly placing all other ethnic groupings under his control. As a result, in the ensuing election the support of the Urhobo leadership went to the Action Party's rivals, the National Council of Nigeria and the Cameroons. The consequences of this preference were to dog the Urhobo throughout the Nigerian Civil War of 1967–70, when they, along with several other minority groupings, were tragically caught in the clash between the two sides.

Okri's fiction makes little direct reference to the local politics of the creeks, nor has he ever commented directly on any of the above issues, which are in any case typical of the region as a whole.[8] Instead, he has given us a number of closely observed accounts of the early Civil War period, when ethnic tensions of an equivalent kind were played out across the broader canvas of the nation. Many of these accounts focus on the divisive effects of language, and of naming in particular.

In the story 'Laughter beneath the Bridge' from *Incidents at the Shrine*, the narrator and his mother, who are fleeing from the hostilities, are stopped at a road block. The soldier in charge, a federal officer, interrogates the mother in an effort to elicit whether she is an Igbo, and hence a rebel. To test her background and presumed loyalty, he commands her to recite the paternoster in her mother tongue. She evades his enquiry by reciting the prayer in her husband's. After they have been released, she explains to her son, 'They shoot people who can't speak their language' (*IS* 9).

Back at the village, the boy's constant companion Monica is detained by sentries whilst she is crossing a bridge. The sentries want to know where she is from so that they can label her ethnic group. Their probing takes the form of linguistic interrogation: ' "Speak your language!" the soldier shouted as her thighs quivered. "Speak your language!" he screamed as she urinated down her thighs and shivered in her own puddle. She wailed. Then she jabbered. In her language.' The sentries take her away (*IS* 21).

In the first paragraph of the story 'Words that Flourish' from *Stars of the New Curfew*, also set in the early months of a national emergency, the anonymous narrator experiences an encounter with an officious colleague.

> I was at work one day [he tells us] when a man came up to me and asked my name. For some reason I couldn't tell it to him immediately and he didn't wait for me to get around to it before he turned and walked away. At lunchtime I went to the bukka to eat. When I got back to my desk someone told me that half the workers in the department had been sacked. I was one of them. (*SNC* 13)

After his dismissal, the narrator stays at home watching as the growing crisis empties the streets. 'That', he informs us at the climax of his anxiety, 'was when I discovered I had temporarily lost the names of things' (*SNC* 21). He becomes delirious, crazed by linguistic vertigo. 'My head', he confesses, 'jostled with signs'. He gets into his car and escapes from the city. Even then he is tormented by language, fearing his name and identity are inscribed on his features for all to see. A thunderstorm breaks out: 'A moment later there was a forked, incandescent flash of lightning which lit up the handwriting on my face' (*SNC* 24). Reaching his home town, he experiences a communal rite of reintegration. A woman invites him to a ceremony. 'Who are you?' I asked. The woman does not say. That night he attends a meeting at which the villagers recite 'a long list of names' (*SNC* 30). We never discover his.

THE TAPESTRY OF STORIES

The fugue and reticence in these stories are characteristic of Okri's work as a whole, a highly personal art that has gone public.[9] Indeed, Okri's stories frequently appear to be as concerned to elude classification as are their characters. 'Poets', he exhorts his fellow practitioners at the end of the essay 'When the World Sleeps', 'do not let them define you or confine you . . .' (*WBF* 14).

Some definitions are harder to shake off than others. Consider, for example, the label of 'postcoloniality' that has proved so popular in academic circles since the publication of Ashcroft, Griffiths, and Tiffin's critical survey *The Empire Writes Back* of 1987.[10] Used to indicate a critical perspective, this is a term that could profitably be applied, for example, to Okri's own analyses of Shakespeare (*WBF* 71–87). Its limitations become clear when it is employed as a chronological marker. Arguably, the stage in historical evolution identified by the prefix 'post-' can never adequately account for an author who has always been at pains to stress the immemorial roots of his work. As frequently employed, moreover, the adjective 'post-colonial' implies an *anti*-colonial stance too absolute for Okri's writing, which, though it emphatically rebuts imperialism, does so in a unique and nuanced way.

Similar objections apply to two other tags that have been tied too often and too crudely onto Okri's work: 'postmodernity' and 'magic realism'. He has accepted neither, and has on occasions been brusque at the expense of 'well-meaning scholars', 'guardsmen' of 'the ivory tower' who employ such jargon too glibly (*WBF* 70). 'Words that conceal, words that reduce': such commonplaces name Okri's work; they do not describe it. I once asked Okri what he thought of the magic realist school, and of the fiction of Gabriel García Márquez in particular. 'It's all right,' he replied non-committally. 'But you know what it amounts to in the end?' With weary tolerance he droned down the telephone line the quaint but repetitious melody of Ravel's interminable *Boléro*.

In an essay in the collection *A Way of Being Free*, 'Newton's Child', Okri has this to say about certain kinds of intellectual subtlety: 'Better a complex mind behind a seemingly simple thought, than a simple mind behind a seemingly complex thought. The mind should surround what it expresses' (*WBF* 20). The trouble with all of the aforementioned terms as applied to Okri is that they tend to absorb his texts into a hegemonic discourse, or set of discourses. Furthermore, these

9

concepts are too ambitious for the writer's expressive, and the reader's receptive, mind to be able to 'surround'. The title of Okri's Newton essay refers to a passage in Sir David Brewster's *Memoirs* of the great seventeenth-century scientist. In it Brewster quotes the ageing mathematician's words as he looks back on a lifetime's achievements as a theorist. The original passage runs: 'I do not know what I may appear to the world, but to myself I seem only to have been a boy playing on the sea-shore, and diverting myself in now and then finding a smoother pebble or a prettier shell than ordinary, whilst the great ocean of truth lay undiscovered all before me.'[11]

The terms postcoloniality, postmodernity, and magic realism are wonderfully smooth to the touch. They are also exceptionally pretty. Their limitation is that they aspire to name the ocean.

The reliance of some critics on these conventional indicators is regrettable, since Okri has provided some far more appropriate signposts of his own. In his piece on Newton, for example, he speaks of 'the law of visuality' and 'the law of subliminal effect' (*WBF* 24). In the second part of a later essay, 'The Joys of Storytelling' – a set of three interlocked meditations on the potentiality of fiction – he talks of 'compacted narratives' and 'tangential narratives' (*WBF* 68). I shall also have reason to speak of 'delayed recognition' (p. 77), 'reversed bathos' (p. 78), 'migrating consciousness' (p. 78), 'converging circles' (p. 79), and the law of 'inverted mimesis' (p. 81). None of these phrases is intended to label or identify cultural or literary movements to which Okri belongs. Instead, they enshrine propositions about technique.

Okri has more to say about this matter in his novel *Infinite Riches*, where he introduces an alternative social commentator to his purblind colonial governor. She is an old woman living in the fastness of the forest who is busily engaged weaving a 'tapestry of stories' (*IR* 105–6). Her handiwork depicts the history of her nation, and of all nations. Everything and everybody appears in its fanciful design: Azaro, his mother and father, Madame Koto, the misguided governor. The woman's cloth expounds a vibrant but also a slightly sinister narrative that encloses past, present, and future. At night she sleeps beneath it; when Azaro and his dad discovers her in a forest clearing, 'her presence was a mood of a thousand stories' that leave them bewildered and exhausted.

This gifted woman is a practitioner of an ambivalent craft that Okri identifies in the third part of 'The Joys of Storytelling' as the making and unmaking of nations, and of the world (*WBF* 109; 119–20). Progressive nations, he there reminds us, make up progressive stories; regressive nations tell themselves regressive tales. A story can corrupt a people or redeem it. Arguably the continent of Africa has too many competing stories, and is waiting for some grand narrative integration. In any case, all cultures possess stories, and there is a surprising similarity between them. Indeed, the capacity of narrative to transcend cultural barriers, to body forth in fiction the aspirations of the whole of humanity, is one of its most encouraging qualities. But, wherever and however they occur, stories are the opposite of names, because they distil a transforming capacity possessed by events and people that is forever carrying them beyond any possible nomenclature.

These clues and messages are encoded into Okri's work, lying for much of the time in its concealed and secret places. A true critique of his art will, therefore, pay as much attention to its deep as to its surface structures. Some of its most illuminating insights are so subtly implicit as to be almost invisible to the tabulating sight or mind. If Okri's writing is to be understood aright, it must, I believe, be viewed in relation to certain key conceptions: about stories as receptacles of meaning, and about the relationship in all art between the seen and the unseen, the evident and the unsuspected.

In an aphorism in 'The Joys of Storytelling III' that almost cites the title of one of his own novels, Okri sets forth a 'challenge for our age, and future ages'. It is 'to do for storytelling what Joyce did for language – to take it to its highest levels of enchantment and magic; to impact into story infinite richness and convergences' (*WBF* 111). With this destination in view, with just such a faith in the piloting power of narratives, Okri's work moves like Eneke the bird, not perching but flying.

11

2

Among the Spirit Children, 1959–1978

Heclipses hate children. They eat them.

(Ben Okri, 'In the Shadow of War')

Behold how great a matter a little fire kindleth!

(Epistle of James, 3: 5)

The town of Minna on the central Nigerian plateau owes its colonial and postcolonial prominence to one fact. It is here that the railway line from the former capital Lagos passes before joining the track from Port Harcourt, commercial hub of the country's oil-rich east, to contine its journey northwards towards Kano and the sub-Saharan savannah. For decades Minna has attracted workers from all over this disparate nation. It was here in September 1921 that the novelist Cyprian Ekwensi, author of *People of the City* and *Jaguar Nana*, was born to Igbo-speaking parents. It was here too that, on Sunday, 15 March 1959, a son Benjamin was born to Silver Oghenegueke Loloje Okri, an Urhobo from near Warri in the delta region, then employed by the Nigeria Railway Corporation, and his wife, Grace, an Igbo from the Mid-West.

Ben's Okri's antecedents on both sides are of interest. The Mid-Western or delta Igbos, his mother's people, possess an identity quite distinct from that of the Igbos further east, about whom the Ogidi-born Achebe has memorably written. Okonwo, contumacious hero of *Things Fall Apart*, and Ezeulu, priestly protagonist of his *Arrow of God*, inhabit a meritocratic society of palavers, councils, and painstakingly acquired titles.[1] The delta Igbo, by contrast, have derived an aristocratic kinship system and habit of mind from the former Benin Empire to the north, of which they were once suzerains. Grace Okri, the youngest of seven sisters, was from a direct chiefly line – 'an Igbo princess', a 'spiritual dove', is how Ben has lovingly described her. I met her several times: a bountiful and quietly sustaining presence. Silver Okri, for his part, descended less directly – through a great-grandfather on his mother's side – from one Urhobo royal clan. To Ben he was to come to seem 'stoic', 'Roman'. Through this complicated inheritance, heroism, and grace too, flow in the blood.

Minna is not an exotic place: it is Nigeria's Swindon or, more properly, its Crewe. In the mind of a very small child whose parents spoke of homes elsewhere, it was, nonetheless, bizarre enough. Not long after learning to walk, Ben remembers getting lost there, though in his description of the incident the place is hard to recognize. He went 'wondering in a strange town in north Nigeria ... walking lost ... wandering away from home. I was in a strange town amongst complete strangers. But I was completely at ease and I mysteriously found my way to my uncle's place. I was not disturbed at all as I wandered through the town.'[2] The resemblance of this recollection to some scene from *The Famished Road* is as illuminating about that book as it is revealing of the state of mind of the wandering – and wondering – child.

This infant had a younger brother called independent Nigeria, brought into being with the unfurling of a flag and the braying of a band on 1 October 1960, sixteen months and sixteen days after its elder sibling. The fact that the various cultures composing this fledgling nation are both immeasurably old and dangerously diverse should not be allowed to disguise the significance of this event. In 1960 Nigeria was the largest, richest, and most vocal nation in anglophone black Africa. Silver and Grace came from two different minority groups within it. Silver, for one, was not tempted by any of the paths to success accessible to some more favourably placed people (for Yorubas, perhaps the Civil Service or academic life; for Hausas and northerners generally, the army). Because of the uneven distribution of educational opportunities in colonial Nigeria, the Urhobo did not at the time enjoy their fair share of graduates and lawyers. In any case, the most attractive avenue to self-advancement for citizens with rights to defend lay through the legal profession.

So in 1961 Silver Okri sailed to London to read and 'eat his dinners' in preparation for the bar exams at the Inner Temple. Several months into his course he was joined by his family: eventually three boys and a girl. The Okris settled in south-east London, in shabby genteel Peckham. The previous year the Scottish novelist Muriel Spark had set her macabre comedy of lower-middle class-manners, *The Ballad of Peckham Rye* (1960), about a mile to the south of them. The Okris though settled in north Peckham, not far from Lugard Road, named after the first colonial governor of Nigeria, and just round the corner from Queens Road station, from which, conveniently for a law student, trains ran twice an hour to the terminus at London Bridge. To keep the family finances afloat, and to fund his studies, Silver Okri worked part-time in a Camberwell launderette.

From September 1964, aged 5, Ben attended John Donne Primary School at the corner of Woods Road and Harders Road.[3] The school was named after the celebrated seventeenth-century metaphysical poet and Dean of St Paul's Cathedral. Ben's reading at the time, however, inclined more towards the *Beano* comic, the daredevil hero of whose weekly strip cartoon, Dennis the Menace, he and his classmates much admired. He joined a street gang modelling its behaviour on the escapades of this short-trousered tearaway, which included letting down the tyres of parked cars. By his own reckoning Ben was one of two black children then attending John Donne, too small a proportion to cause serious cultural tension. One January afternoon, some of his fellow students started to lob snowballs at him. It was probably an invitation to horseplay, though he suspected some ill intent. Silver, come to collect his son at the school gates, told him not to retaliate.

In July 1965 Silver Okri was called to the bar[4] and soon sailed for Africa with his family. The member least enthusiastic to leave was Ben, who had to be coaxed onto the departing liner by one of Grace's stratagems. She assured the 6 year old that he needed to stay aboard only long enough to say goodbye to his departing relations.[5] When the boy looked out of the porthole, the docks were moving.

The Okris arrived three weeks later to find a nation coming apart. When they had left Nigeria, it was a nation within the Commonwealth divided into four regions. It was now a republic, with much of the education and expertise located in the south and east, but most of the power remaining in the Islamic north. Already, the Yoruba Prime Minister of the Western Region, Chief Obafemi Awolowo, had fallen foul of the national government, which had imprisoned him for attempting to undermine the constitution. In January 1966 the federal Prime Minister, Sir Abubakar Tafawa Balewa, a northerner, had been assassinated by a group of junior army officers, who seized power. People in the south were restless. In February, a group of 150 young men calling themselves 'the Delta Volunteer Force' had proclaimed a Niger Delta Republic. It had been suppressed after twelve days. Within a few weeks an Igbo soldier, Major-General Johnson Aguiyi-Ironsi, had emerged as the leader of the new national government. Believing that prevailing arrangements reinforced the imbalance between the various parts of the country, he was now attempting to introduce a single, unitary constitution. A popular move in some quarters, this was much resented in others.

On Friday, 22 July 1966, Silver Okri was enrolled as a member of the Nigerian bar.[6] A week later, on Friday, 27 July, Aguiyi-Ironsi was murdered in a second *coup* and replaced by a northerner, Lieutenant General Yakubu Gowon. Ethnic tension reached fever pitch in September and October when the Hausa-speaking majority in the northern city of Kano turned against the resident Igbo population, massacring 30,000. Rumours of retaliations taken against northerners living in Port Harcourt exacerbated feelings further. By the end of the year Lieutenant Colonel Ojukwu had emerged as the leader of Igbo hardliners who felt that the Eastern Region must break away from the federation. In January 1967 all attempts at arbitration failed when a conference between easterners and the Lagos government, held in the mountains above Ghana's capital Accra, reached an agreement that Gowon would not implement. On 30 May, Ojukwu announced the secession of the autonomous state of Biafra. Two months later, the Nigerian Civil War had begun.

The outbreak of hostilities split the country's intelligentsia down the middle. After some soul searching, Achebe quitted Lagos for the Biafran capital Enugu, where he took a post with the Biafran Ministry of Information. His friend and fellow Igbo, the poet Christopher Okigbo – a figure to whom Okri, 8 at the time, has always felt strongly drawn – had already written a set of jeremiads 'prophesying war'. He now resigned his position with the Cambridge University Press in Ibadan and enlisted in the Biafran army as a major. When Okigbo perished on the field of battle in Nsukka in August 1967, Biafra had acquired its most illustrious literary martyr. Non-Igbos went a number of ways over the issue (as, let it be said, did some Igbos). The novelist Elechi Amadi fought in the federal army, whilst the author Ken Saro-Wiwa, an Ogoni, accepted from the Lagos administration the minor post of the governorship of Bonny island, recaptured from the Biafrans in July. In contrast, the dramatist Wole Soyinka, a Yoruba who regarded the war as a squabble between politicians that could do the common people nothing but harm, visited Ojukwu's capital to set up a 'Third Force' between the contending parties. On his return westwards, Soyinka was arrested by the federal authorities and held prisoner for a little over two years in Ibadan, Lagos, and Kaduna.[7]

The war thus effectively demonstrated a lesson that Okri himself was to learn more intimately: at times of national stress, writers and thinkers are in trouble, whatever they say, and whichever way they turn. The road of the conciliators was as hard as – if not harder than – that of partisans. For ordinary inhabitants of Nigeria or Biafra the new state of affairs was also confusing and alarming. Few people wanted war, though none could ignore it. In effect, the hostilities represented a special instance of that futility in naming that we discussed in the previous chapter. The position of the Urhobo was especially difficult. The short-lived delta republic had already made clear the political instability of the creeks. Now that the Biafrans had broken away, the Urhobos and Ijos were reluctant to join them for fear of being dominated once more, this time within a smaller political unit. Recognizing this, the Lagos authorities soon made overtures, hoping that the Mid-Westerners' instinctive distrust of Ojukwu's fledgling state could be turned to federal advantage. It was a situation in which any decision might prove fatal.

There was no easy path. Silver decided to build a house and a law practice in one of the more run-down areas of Lagos. The atmosphere of the place can be gleaned from Okri's, evocation, towards the end of his first novel, *Flowers and Shadows*, and in his second, *The Landscapes Within*, of the comparable district of Alaba. Situated between Victoria Island and the opulent suburb of Ikoyi, Alaba is the site of Lagos's principal electricity market, a bustling commercial area where many of the traders are Igbos. In *Flowers and Shadows* the narrator describes it as a vital if grubby place. In its exhilarating though shabby ambience, it is akin to the quarter where Okri grew up.

Living in such an environment was a lesson in social adaptation and the saving graces of the imagination. 'Ghetto-dwellers are the great fantasists,' Okri later declared. 'The ghetto was the place I've felt most at home because the terms on which everyone lives are so transparent. There is one code. Survival – but survival with honour and style. There was an extraordinary vibrancy there, an imaginative life. When you are that poor, all you've got left is your belief in the imagination.'[8] The Lagos of Okri's novels in fact bears much the same relationship to its original as the London of *Oliver Twist* to the nineteenth-century metropolis, or Muriel Spark's Peckham to the environs of Rye Lane in the 1960s. It is, in other words, magnified, intensified, rendered mystical. A prime example of this process is the pond of green slime lying in the road outside the young painter-protagonist's house in *The Landscapes Within*. The poorer areas of West African cities abound in such stagnant pools. When Omovo depicts it with his vivid pigments, it becomes a veritable lake of corruption, 'a large vanishing scumscape' (*LW* 33; *IR* 26).

From Lagos Ben travelled to boarding school, initially to the Children's Home School in Sapele, a port town on the River Ethiope, fifty miles up the road to Benin city from Silver's home town of Warri. Though normally a quiet rural spot, it was in 1967 as little sheltered from the realities of war as any other part of the south. Indeed, few parts of the country were more affected by the chaos of fighting than the Mid-West, an area that both Silver and Grace regarded as home, but that now lay in the path between the two sides. In the early months of the conflict, the Biafran army marched on Warri and Benin, briefly capturing both. After the Biafrans had been repulsed, the federal forces – 'gallant troops' as the Lagos newspapers invariably described them – fought their way in the opposite direction, but along much the same route. The road of advance towards Ojukwu's capital lay via Benin city, fifty miles to the north of Sapele, then due east over Onitscha Bridge, a strategically important thoroughfare joining the towns of Asaba and Onitscha across the Niger and its tributary the Anambra. The bridge was traversed and re-traversed several times by detachments of competing loyalty between 1967 and 1970.

As Ben studied, warplanes growled overhead. Around him, enclave after enclave changed hands, while the terrified and bewildered populace fended as best it could. The local Igbo-speaking population, Grace's kinsfolk, were especially vulner-able. Having felt at a disadvantage to the eastern Igbos in the former Eastern Region, they, like the Urhobos, had been reluctant to entrust their destiny to breakaway Biafra, or even to endorse the secession. Regarded by the Biafrans as traitors, by the federal forces as enemies, they fled or hid. Atrocities against civilians were common. The most frequent images of the war observed on black-and-white television screens in faraway Europe were of pot-bellied children in an increasingly isolated Biafra, interdispersed with shots of stately, white-robed northerners astride horses. For the local population, a more familiar sight was of the broken and mutilated bodies of civilians or soldiers sprawled by the roadside, beneath bridges or under trees. 'My education took place simultaneously with my relations being killed,' remembers Okri, 'and friends who one day got up in class and went out to fight the war'.[9] For children, especially those of mixed parentage, the blood-soaked scenario was bewildering. This was the case even for those who did not observe carnage at close quarters. Many children, of course, did so.

Soon Ben was moved to the relative safety of Christ's High School in the university city of Ibadan, 100 miles inland from Lagos. Meanwhile under relentless federal pressure abetted by Britain and other western powers, Biafra shrank to a malnourished enclave, as Enugu, Port Harcourt, Aba, and then Umuahia fell.[10] Hostilities came to an end in January 1970 with the reintegration of Biafra into Gowon's Nigeria.

Slowly social life returned to normal. Nothing could obliterate the memory. The war produced a psychological and cultural aftermath, to which Okri's earliest fiction arguably belongs. The protagonists in these stories are often Okri's contemporaries. Few of them have fought in the war, but all have been affected by it in perceptible ways. These are men and women traumatized by conflict to whom memories of a violent past are forever returning unbidden. All of these characters, furthermore, are acutely conscious of the fragility of the social order around them. Chaos is always within mental – and usually within physical – reach. In Okri's apprentice writing these factors – though beautifully observed – seem dismal, even depressing. The achievement of his later work has been to give similar material the dimensions of epic.

He can only have been made more aware of the complexities of the national situation when at 11 he went eastwards to Urhobo College in Warri. The delta region was now officially at peace, and the local economy was increasingly dominated by international oil companies that had moved into the area to exploit its fossil fuel reserves. In the title story to his collection *Stars of the New Curfew*, Okri records the atmosphere: 'It was a town with a history of slave trading, a town of bad dreams, surrounded by creeks and forests of palm-trees, and rubber plantations. It had become a centre of excitement only on account of its abundance of oil wells' (*SNC* 111). Notices from the petroleum companies had sprung up everywhere, and the social divide between those who had benefited from the new wealth and those who had not was as broad as the River Warri that slunk through the town. The resulting fractiousness, and the thin veneer of *nouveau riche* snobbery lying like a glossy film of petrol over the endemic poverty, are powerfully portrayed in Okri's story. Urhobo College itself had been a pioneering institution, founded in the late 1940s by the officials of the Urhobo Progress Union in an attempt to close the educational gap between the Urhobo and their immediate neighbours.[11] It was a focus for tribal aspiration in a tri-ethnic town existing to provide the lawyers, teachers, and civil servants that Silver's people had once so desperately needed. Ben was very aware of the tradition. 'It used', he wrote, 'to be the classic school for those who were to study in their lives the crude mythologies of survival' (*SNC* 110). It cannot have satisfied Ben's growing intellectual curiosity. Leaving in his mid-teens, he took odd jobs in Lagos while swatting for his higher school certificate privately, hoping in the long run to attend a local university to study natural science.

Silver's more effectual contribution to his son's education displayed a certain affectionate guile. He had arranged his library of British classics, acquired in grey and distant London, along a bookcase in the front room of the family's still incomplete Lagos villa. He instructed his children on no account to disturb them. The provocation was well timed, the psychology perfect. Soon Dennis the Menace was nose-deep in English nineteenth-century novels. He emerged with a permanent recognition of the feats words perform by conjuring up worlds. He became a voracious reader: of Dickens and Jane Austen in early years, later of African, continental European, and American novels, of English-language poetry, and poetry in translation.

The impact of Dickens was permanent, and can be detected in Okri's fiction to this day. Much of this writing is generational: that is to say, it reproduces with unforgettable fidelity the relationship between old and young, fathers and sons, in a society passing through rapid urban change. The Jeffia of *Flowers and Shadows*, the Omovo of *The Landscapes Within*, of *Dangerous Love*, and of the story 'In the Shadow of War', the Azaro of 'The Famished Road' sequence, are all blood brothers of Dickens's younger male protagonists: of Oliver Twist – to whom the narrator of the story 'Stars of the New Curfew' fleetingly compares himself (*SNC* 115) – of Nicholas Nickleby, of David Copperfield, and of Pip in *Great Expectations*. The interesting difference is that Dickens for biographical reasons tends to orphan his child characters, whilst Okri for equally profound reasons – not biographical ones – portrays his young protagonists as engaged in a fervent, though only partially acknowledged, involvement with their parents. (Even so, it is arguable that, viewed from certain perspectives, Azaro is *symbolically* an orphan.)

It is worth stressing this fact because, despite superficial coincidences of time and place – both Jeffia and Omovo are Urhobos – the families depicted in these books are very different from Okri's own. The psychology of growth so vividly portrayed in these texts has little to do with personal history. It is, on the other hand, both deep-seated and profoundly literary. The personalities of Okri's young protagonists often seem to hark back to Dickens in particular, being by turns as trusting as Oliver, as gullible as David, as adventurous as Nicholas, or as flawed and as sentimental as Pip.[12] The novels in which they appear, moreover, share a formal quality with Dickens, consisting in a certain instability of grammatical person. I am surely not unique in finding that, between rereadings, it is occasionally difficult to recall whether a particular novel by Dickens is couched in the first- or third-person singular. (*David Copperfield* and *Great Expectations* are in fact in the first person, whereas *Oliver Twist* and *Nicholas Nickleby* are in the third.) 'The Famished Road' sequence, of course, is in the first person with episodes in a reported third. In his first two published novels, Okri lets these two grammatical standpoints flow into one another, employing a normative third-person form with occasional excursions into first-person narrative. As a result, in each case the young male protagonist features both as an observed character and as a soliloquizing self. The versatility is enhancing.

There is a further, related indebtedness to Dickens. Okri's novels and stories tend to revolve about inwardness and crowds. This dichotomy extends far beyond the relationship between the individual and society conventionally discussed when analysing novels of social documentary. Okri's protagonists do not simply merge with, or stand apart from, their societies. They are hemmed in, overlooked, eavesdropped upon to an extent that becomes well-nigh intolerable. In reaction, they are obliged to carve out a psychological and creative space in which they can be themselves. A room of one's own is a relative luxury in most African cities, and Lagos is no exception. In many of Okri's stories the principal character, a paradigm of the artist whether he recognizes it or not, guards and nourishes his independence with precocious determination, while managing to keep the wider community

– even the community of the family – at a tactful, subtly manipulated distance. All of these tales evoke congestion, and all concentrate on solitude. The problems that they indicate are products of poverty and economic need; they also dig deeper into the origins and imaginative cohesion of cities, and the constitution of the imaginative, transformational self. They are, furthermore, indicative of the extent to which Okri, like his admired Dickens, is essentially an urban – even a metropolitan – writer.

Ben has often described the moment when he turned to writing. He had been working as a lowly paid clerk in the commercial division of ICI, struggling every morning onto the local molue buses to get to work, then returning at night by the same exhausting means. During his leisure hours, the well-furnished front room of the Okri house was an oasis of calm:

> On this particular day, everybody was out and I was in, alone. I was sitting in the living room and I took out a piece of paper and drew what was on the mantelpiece. That took me about an hour. Then I took another piece of paper and wrote a poem. The drawing was dreadful and the poem was ... tolerable, bearable. And it became clear to me that this was my more natural area.[13]

He continued writing on the roof of the structurally still incomplete house 'looking down between the spiky metal entrails to the whole of Lagos'.[14] By the age of 17 he was contributing short stories to local newspapers. Several were accepted. As he squeezed between the passengers on the daily trek to work, he would sometimes watch as a fellow commuter pored over a piece of his fiction in the sweaty, agitated crush.

The plan to read science at a local college came to nothing. So Okri decided to try his luck in London, a city of which he possessed the vaguest of recollections. In Autumn 1978 he set off, with the manuscript of a novel entitled *Flowers and Shadows* packed into his hand luggage.

3

Responsibilities: Fictions, 1978–1982

If I don't learn to shut my mouth I'll soon go to hell,
I, Okigbo, town-crier, together with my iron bell.
> (Christopher Okigbo, 'Hurrah for Thunder')

... what the dickens his name is.
> (Shakespeare, *The Merry Wives of Windsor*, III. ii)

Over the last few years Okri's first two novels – *Flowers and Shadows*, written in the mid- to late 1970s, though not published until 1980, and *The Landscapes Within*, issued late the following year – have largely been eclipsed by *The Famished Road* and the books that came after it. It is important to correct this imbalance, partly because these books are of intrinsic worth, and partly because they are the seed from which the later, more confidently original work arose.

Interestingly, each of these works takes hold of an adage or quotation, turns it over in the palm of its hand, and asks, '*Is this true?*'; '*If so, in what sense?*'; '*What, if we pursued this lesson to its logical extent, would the consequences be: for me, for you, for society, for the world?*' Even more promisingly, each novel probes the nature and the limits of stories: what they can and cannot do, the differences between fiction and fantasy, or between both and so-called 'reality'. Both are placed in Africa – in a recognizable Lagos – yet, in a manner typical of this author, neither is consumed by its setting. Its location is a mode of being, one illustration of a set of human responses that run much deeper: at a subterranean, almost a sub-fictive level. Both books, moreover, posit much the same difficult question. What, they ask, does it mean to be responsible: as a citizen, an artist, or, more broadly, as a human being?

Both books describe the lives of young male Lagos dwellers. But Jeffia Okwe, the idealistic only son of a self-made businessman, and Omovo, the dreamy painter from the slums, are altogether different characters facing distinct, if related, problems. *Flowers and Shadows* is a study of privilege. Its young protagonist Jeffia possesses much that is supposed to make life sweet. He is intelligent, well qualified, healthy, even handsome – and he lives with his parents in the opulent district of Ikoyi. By the end of the novel his businessman father and his best friend are both dead, and he has moved with his mother to the less-favoured district of Alaba. This is not because they have failed, nor because Jeffia has had any great mental revelation: resolutions that belong to a different sort of fiction. True, there are epiphanies – 'showings forth' – of a sort in this finely wrought book. But these, as we shall see, are of a subtle variety: the kind maybe that you might achieve by turning over one of the flowers of the title and examining its petals from beneath.

Much can be gleaned from an episode early in the tale, one that is echoed not only elsewhere in the book but also in its immediate successor, and at other moments in Okri's later fiction as well. It describes the tormenting of a 'brown and white puppy' (*FS* 4–6). Jeffia observes this atrocity while strolling back home at night from his schoolfriend Ode's house, where they have been discussing the morality of intervention. The perpetrators are a couple of ragged boys a little younger than Jeffia. His first reaction is to pose a question: 'Why are these boys being cruel to it like that?' Jeffia does not, as many in his position might, condemn the boys vocally or mentally for their callousness. He accepts at face value the younger boy's excuse, delivered in pleading pidgin, 'My father was jailed – they say he thief, what can a poor man do? If man no die, he no rotten'. Jeffia looks no further into this half-explained misery: he is not a revolutionary, social analyst, or animal-rights activist. Unconsciously, nonetheless, he recognizes the psychology behind the cruelty: 'he understood that those who knew pain lived pain.' He also instinctively knows what he can do to ease the dog's suffering. After a brief and playful bargaining, he buys the animal and takes it home.

This transaction assumes for Jeffia the aspect of a compassionate adventure, whose wider implications he only partially admits to. Yet the episode also disturbs him quite deeply. He is disoriented by it, just as he is by the sight of a man idly throwing stones at nesting birds, whom he observes a few pages further on (*FS* 20). This is the first of a series of parallels or sequels to the dog-tormenting episode that recur in the story. The puppy turns out to belong to Juliet, one of the discarded mistresses of Jeffia's father, Jonan. When, having elicited that she is the owner as a result of a newspaper advertisement, Jeffia visits her to return her pet, an unsuspected aspect of his father's squalid past is laid bare. The dog molesting is also obliquely connected to Jonan in quite a different way, through the younger tormentor's claim that his father has been framed for theft. This is more or less what has happened to the father of Cynthia, the young nurse with whom Jeffia takes up halfway through the narrative. In this instance, it is a commercial agent of Jonan's who has performed the framing. Juliet, Cynthia's father – indirectly Cynthia as well – the dog-harassing urchins of that early scene: all feature as victims. In every case the source of their discomfiture turns out to lie uncomfortably close to Jeffia himself.

These diverse strands in the plot combine to raise an essential and unifying question: the nature in this – or indeed in any – society of moral and civic responsibility. Why, the book seems to ask, is life like this, and who – or what – is to blame? The text offers no simple answer. At moments indeed, the writing almost gives the impression of passively accepting a destiny that nobody can control. It sustains this almost-attitude partly through Jeffia's behaviour, an 'unintentional indifference' (*FS* 119), which at times seems non-judgemental almost to a fault. It reinforces this sense of helplessness through a series of unhappy flukes, the causes of which lie beyond strict personal accountability. The most obvious case is the death early on of Ode, crushed by a lorry whose driver has not heard the young man's cries. Jeffia's reaction to this tragedy – like his mother's – is to call it 'unbelievable'. The adjective may mean that they both consider the lorry driver to have been incredibly negligent; their general attitude, however, suggests that they regard the accident as another example of a malevolent – or indifferent – fate (*FS* 72).

The impression of cosmic powerlessness is beautifully underscored at points by images of psychedelic intensity. Two recur in quick succession in chapters fourteen and fifteen. The first describes a run-over dog, its entrails spread luridly across the road (*FS* 124), a symbol clearly connected with the dog-hurting incident at the beginning. The second describes a baby beetle stranded in the garden of Jeffia's house while tiny ants swarm all over it (*FS* 129). There is a premonition of both these inadvertent deaths earlier in the story. One night, whilst driving home in the dark, Jeffia drives over a frog (*FS* 50). Typically, his reaction is not to question his own driving, but to identify with the amphibian: 'Deep down inside himself. He felt that someone had stepped on his quiet life.' Jeffia observes all of these spectacles of supine suffering with lingering curiosity etched with moral concern. He does not, however, explicitly interpret them as elements within a wider pattern. Is Jeffia therefore deficient?

In vivid contrast to this quietism, there are elements in the book that turn it almost into a detective story, with Jeffia as the industrious sleuth, and his father as the culprit. Jeffia learns quite a lot about his father during the months covered by the action. One lesson – though not I think the most important – is that Jonan's relative success in business has been facilitated by shady dealings that have laid waste everything – and almost everyone – around him. Jonan's victims stretch out endlessly. As well as Juliet and Cynthia's unnamed father there is Sowho, Jonan's estranged half brother. This relation has actively contributed to the commercial success of Jonan's enterprises, but has been cheated out of his share. Jonan lives in fear of his turning up on the doorstep and demanding his cut. When he does so, the resulting car chase kills both men (*FS* 176). Another victim is a former employee who knows too much about the nefarious aspects of the firm. Jonan hires a group of thugs to kill him. Fortuitously his murder leads Jeffia to Cynthia. He observes the assault while driving home, and meets his girlfriend-to-be whilst crouching over the victim's bruised and dying body (*FS* 66).

Various explanations are available for all this visible distress – what Okri in a telling phrase calls 'the unacceptable continuum of the unfortunate' (*FS* 189). Jeffia vacillates between them. The first, and least plausible, is to see all this misery as symptomatic of the corruption and nastiness strangling Nigeria. This is the line taken, for example, by Okri's friend Adewale Maja-Pierce in his introduction to the Longman African Classics edition of the novel. Maja-Pierce views the cumulative suffering in the book as a comment on the venality gripping the country during the oil boom of the 1970s, when Nigeria languished beneath Gowon's military heel. He thus connects the book with a number of 'state-of-the-nation' novels published during this period by writers such as Festus Iyayi, Kole Omotoso, Ifeoma Okoye, and Bode Sowande (*FS* xiii). True, there are satirical scenes that favour this interpretation, notably one that Maja-Pierce cites: an observation of Lagos's soldiery on traffic duty (*FS* 97). Such incidents, though, are few and far between. Their relative scarcity suggests to me that Okri was already a very different kind of novelist from his immediate Nigerian contemporaries.

The second alternative would be to adopt Jeffia's own temperamental quietism by regarding all these phenomena – military thuggishness, commercial malpractice, the suffering of animals – as products of unpitying destiny. At one point Okri underpins this point of view by applying to Ode's untimely death a fragment from the Greek dramatist Menander: 'those whom the gods love, die young.' This received and pessimistic view is occasionally hinted at by Okri's style, over which his sensibility seems not yet to be fully in control. The result is a series of rhetorical, limp-wristed phrases that might be grouped under the heading 'the novel wringing its hands'. Such is the sentence in chapter one about the winds being 'eavesdropping messengers of the gods' (*FS* 7), or the 'hells' in which Cynthia's father is regarded as living, swamping her justified feelings of indignation beneath 'a feeling of futility' (*FS* 82).

The third and most persuasive option is to interpret the action of the novel through its central human relationships: the complementary but very different rapports that Jeffia achieves with his parents. Jonan, after all, is the apparent source of much of the suffering in the book, while his wife, whom he continues commendably to protect, is arguably his most intimate victim. Jeffia's attitudes towards the world are mostly refracted through this double focus. Despite the dispiriting discoveries he comes across during the course of the story, he continues to feel affection for his father. It is an inarticulate love, a baffled love, possibly a remnant from an earlier phase of emotional development, but it is nonetheless intense. Nowhere does this emerge more clearly than in the scene, recognizable to all teenage readers, in which Jonan rails at his son for being out late (FS 69–70). His bluster collapses after a few seconds. Jonan can terrify his employees; his wrath cannot convince his boy. There is an unspoken empathy between them that compels Jonan to be lenient with Jeffia even when his moral meddling almost gets both of them into trouble with the police. As a result, Jeffia can see right through his father's irate front. Like many tyrants, Jonan is fundamentally a weak man. Furthermore, he is culturally confused, espousing modernity whilst furtively communing with *juju* spirits. Maja-Pierce interprets this reliance on traditional remedies as connecting him with evil in some way. Actually – in every available sense – it is viewed as pathetic.

The clue to Jonan's temperament lies in his relationship with his own father, a subsistence farmer from a remote village in Urhoboland who lived a life of near destitution. Eventually Jeffia's grandfather had succumbed to a wasting disease that there was no money to treat. His last words to Jonan were 'My son ... poverty is a curse' (FS 111). The memory of that ignominious end – of his father's 'dying face, crushed and wasted' – haunts Jonan, rushing back to torment him at inconvenient moments. The recollection fills him with 'melancholy', but it also spurs him on. 'It had always been a driving part of his life' comments the narrator. 'It gave him energy.'

Just as Jonan's ruthless pursuit of business success is motivated by his father's economic failure, so his wife's tenacity, her loyalty, maternal instincts, and touching trust, are products of insecurities in her own very different background. An orphan, she has been abused mentally and physically as a child and a young woman. Jonan has rescued her from a destructive earlier relationship, and given her the warmth, material comfort, and self-respect she so desperately craved. Unsurprisingly she is devoted to him, and their only child is the apple of her eye. Through her we perceive a different Jonan, a person for whom the 'state-of-the-nation' version of the story – or the opposed fatalistic reading – have no room: someone affectionate, practical, and, in the private realm at any rate, pretty effective.

In essence, Jonan is a decent man undermined by a combination of his own history and of economic circumstances. A vital clue to his mental make-up – and to the novel's theme of social inequity – occurs in chapter twelve when a beggar who has materialized out of the crowd in downtown Lagos attempts to clean the windscreen of his chauffeur-driven Mercedes with a cloth. The beggar is a picture of destitution, 'a travesty of a man' (*FS* 100), and the rag is filthy. Jonan buys him off with a hastily flung naira note, yet all the way back to the office his face remains 'screwed up'. With precocious restraint, Okri refrains from telling us why this is so. It is left for the reader to work out that the beggar represents everything the plutocrat loathes and dreads. He is the man Jonan fears he might have become.

With uncanny insight, Jeffia understands much of this. His insight partly explains the tentativeness – as well as the affability – of his filial nature. It also enables him to contemplate the significance of the second Mosaic commandment with its well-known corollary 'for the sins of the fathers are visited upon the children'. Jeffia's preoccupation with this adage is of a kind with the quiet pessimism of his personality, but it also transcends it. The 'sin', if you remember your Exodus, was idolatry.[1] Jonan is not altogether a sinner, and the danger of Jeffia being swamped by his legacy is, I think, offset by his shrewdness. Nevertheless, it is before the idol of Mammon that Jonan has bowed. Like his biblical near-namesake Jonah, he has been swallowed up.

The advantage of this critical approach to the novel is that it enables us to construe it as a generational tragedy in the style of Chinua Achebe, rather than a surface satire – or diatribe – after the school of Omotoso or Ijayi. The brittle heroism of Okonkwo, protagonist of Achebe's first novel *Things Fall Apart*, one remembers, was a reaction against the comparative ineffectiveness of his father, the gentle, flute-playing Unoka.[2] *Flowers and Shadows* harks back to such influences, but it also anticipates Okri's later fiction. In chapter fifteen, for example, Jeffia recalls Ode and himself participating in a school debate on international capitalism, environmental vandalism, and racial politics (*FS* 131–2). The discussion looks right forward to the story 'Stars on the New Curfew' in the volume of that title, and to Okri's sixth novel, *Infinite Riches*.

The mutual indebtedness of Okri's books, and the organic coherence of his evolving *œuvre*, are even clearer in his second novel, the book reissued in revised form in 1996 as *Dangerous Love*, but which originally appeared in 1981 under the title *The Landscapes Within*.[3] Okri was just 21 when in March 1980 he finished writing this first version, in which, he later declared, he had wanted to celebrate 'the small details of life as well as the great' and 'to be faithful to life as lived in the round, and yet to tell a worthwhile story' (*DL* 325). As he later saw it, such aims were too ambitious for his skill at the time. Hence the revision. However, the first version richly repays analysis. In it, Okri was to confess, 'I came to see . . . the key to much of my past work, and perhaps also to my future.'

Like *Flowers and Shadows*, *Landscapes Within* begins with a premonition (*LW* 3), this time in the form of two dreams (reduced to one in *DL* 1), the first of which features a murdered girl. These nightmares – recounted in the notebook of the artist-hero Omovo – themselves relate to a series of horrific recalls of the Nigerian Civil War by several characters in the book. Their further significance remains unexplored until chapter seven, when the protagonist Omovo goes walking with his friend Keme along a moonlit Lagos beach (*LW* 54–60; *DL* 43–7). They find the corpse of a girl who has been murdered and mutilated in some kind of perverted rite. Later on, the dream prognostication is fulfilled once again when Omovo's girlfriend Ifeyinwa is killed, as a result partly of mistaken identity, partly of an ongoing tribal tiff, during a return trip to her village (*LW* 265); in *Dangerous Love* she is called 'Ifeyiwa' and her death is related even more starkly (*DL* 281–2). Like the girl in Omovo's dream, all of these women are victims. As in the previous novel, we are prompted to enquire, of what or of whom?

Omovo, who lives in Alaba with his drunken, woebegone father and his resentful stepmother Blackie, makes an unsatisfactory living as a junior clerk in a chemicals firm, from which he is eventually sacked. His passion and vocation, however, are painting (the 'dangerous love' to which the title of the 1996 revision partially alludes). It may be significant that Okri, a one-time employee of ICI, had once toyed with the idea of taking up art as a career. In any case, throughout the book painting serves as a metaphor for all art forms, including literature. An important theme throughout is *mimesis*, or the representation of reality. What, the novel seems to enquire, is the exact relationship between the representation of the world observed in art forms, dreams, fantasies, and the everyday world that we perceive around us? Are art and dream and fantasy all distortions? If so, are they the *same kind* of distortion?

Omovo completes several paintings during the course of the story, one of which is stolen, another lost, and yet another confiscated by the authorities. The most startling, *Drift*, depicts a large pool of stagnant water festering outside his house (*LW* 33; *DL* 26). The intensification of reality in this work has already been alluded to (p. 17). The text here refers to its 'oblique shapes and heads with intent and glittering eyes.' 'He knew now what he wanted,' the narrative adds, 'and he was pleased.' But, when the painting is exhibited at the local 'Ebony' art gallery, the military authorities confiscate it because they think it presents an unflattering impression of Nigeria (*LW* 50; *DL* 39–40). This provocative action is important because, though overbearing, insensitive, and philistine, it is not strictly speaking irrational. In essence, the authorities espouse a Stalinist understanding of art as *agitprop*. For them art is tolerable only if it endorses the official policies of the state. Yet that is also a classical, Platonic view. For the Greek philosopher Plato, artists were of two kinds: those who praised the ideals espoused by the rulers, and those who insisted on representing wickedness. The former were to be supported by the government. The latter, on the other hand, were likely to unsettle the citizens by saying, or perhaps painting, inconvenient things. To prevent this happening, Socrates – Plato's mouthpiece in *The Republic* – demands that they quit the city.[4]

Omovo then is in good company. But so one might say – playing devil's advocate for a moment – is the government.

When feeling discouraged, Omovo strolls round to visit a friend and mentor of his, an older artist named Dr Okocha. It is Okocha who provides a middle road in the argument about art and life – and incidentally encapsulates many of the themes of the novel – by quoting the statement 'In dreams begin responsibilities' (*LW* 118; *DL* 101). Dr Okocha attributes these suggestive words to 'an Indian poet'; in fact they make up the second epigraph to the volume *Responsibilities* (1918) by the Irish poet, W. B. Yeats.[5] No source has been found for this quotation; the current opinion among scholars is that the words are Yeats's own. Yet this paradoxical formulation distils the predicament of many artists in Ireland, Nigeria, or any other postcolonial state. Artists, as both Okocha and Omovo are aware, can operate effectively only through a process of free association, a controlled self-disorientation akin to dreaming (in *Dangerous Love*, Okocha prefers the term 'visions'). In many cases they induce this condition in themselves consciously and deliberately. Others – critics pre-eminently – interpret the effect as they will, but it is hopelessly naive of the originator to disclaim all responsibility for the result. Thus the confiscating authorities were quite justified in asking Omovo 'Why did you do that painting?' (*LW* 50). But Omovo himself was both strictly within his rights – but also somewhat ingenuous – when he replied, 'I just did it. I painted what I had to paint.'

There is a parallel to be drawn here with a novel that Omovo is desultorily reading throughout the story: Wole Soyinka's 1965 study of post-independence manners, *The Interpreters*.[6] That book too centres on a painter, Kola, who is working on a group portrait of several of his friends, all of whom are characters in the plot. Kola has associated each one of these acquaintances visually with an *orisa*, one of the deities of the traditional Yoruba pantheon. His canvas is viewed by Soyinka as a vision – or, as the title of the book implies, an *interpretation* – of the Nigeria of the time, a period some thirteen years before that covered by *The Landscapes Within*. The difference between Kola and Omovo is that the first is quite conscious of what he is doing, whereas Omovo seems to have drifted into his role as social interpreter with a sort of awe-struck insouciance. Why then is he so threatening?

One clue is given in a passage where Omovo is telling Keme about an episode during his childhood when his beloved mother scolded him for staring too hard at a cobweb:

> When I was young, I can't remember how old, I remember my mother beating me with a comb and then with the heel of her shoe. She beat me because I sat for a long time staring at a mass of cobwebs and trying to draw them. She was afraid of cobwebs and said that there was something wrong with me and why should I look at something as strange as a cobweb. I looked at cobwebs and things not only to draw them but to know them. Too many people are afraid to look at cobwebs and other things. That's the problem. (LW 153–4; DL 152)

The interesting aspect of this reminiscence is the different perspective on reality possessed by mother and child. The mother's reprimand is a product of fear and incomprehension, but she is also convinced that the child is actively drawn to nastiness, a perverse preference that she attempts to beat out of him. Yet the growing Omovo, like his older self, is drawn to the unkempt and unsightly facets of his world not because they are out-of-bounds but, as he tells Keme, simply in order to *know* them, to absorb their essence, to interpret their nature, perhaps as a preliminary to painting – or here drawing – them. For Omovo the conventional distinction between beauty and ugliness – an evaluative assessment quite irrelevant to artistic representation as he understands it – simply does not exist. If his mother makes one kind of mistake in construing his motives, the authorities make a second. They assume that Omovo's concentration on the less seemly aspects of social reality – stagnant pools, cobwebs, traffic jams – is a form of criticism. It is not intended as such. Omovo fastens on these sights because they possess a rich visual potential. Above all, he depicts them simply because they exist.

If there is one characteristic that Omovo shares with Jeffia from *Flowers and Shadows*, it is his innocence. Like Jeffia, he has a tendency to accept everything around him with passivity laced with mild curiosity. This, for example, is the attitude that he adopts to the drastic haircut received at the hands of an apprentice barber at the beginning of the book (*LW* 6–7; *DL* 5). Omovo drifts off to sleep and, while he is dozing, the hairdresser cuts off more hair than expected. Jolted into consciousness, Omovo observes the result with interest. In a mood of playful experimentation, he urges the man to continue until he is bald. For the rest of the book Omovo's bare and shining scalp is the subject of intrigued derision by everyone else in the compound. He does not anticipate this reaction; he accepts it nonetheless. In a sense he regards the resulting social obloquy as a new and unaccustomed element in his existence, something of which, like the cobwebs and traffic jams, he must take intelligent account, simply to know it for what it is.

It is this kind of ethical neutrality, viewed by others as amoral, that constantly lands Omovo in trouble, both with the powers-that-be and with his prying, judgemental neighbours. The clash of values is exacerbated when, with a typical lack of foresight, Omovo drifts into an adulterous affair with Ifi, the young country-bred wife of his middle-aged neighbour, Takpo. It is Ifi who enacts yet another parallel with *Flowers and Shadows* when she rescues a lame stray dog from the unwelcome attentions of passers-by (*LW* 228–9, *DL* 228–9). Like so many of the characters in that earlier book, she too is a victim, a product of a broken home whose misery has given her an insight into the sufferings of others. She is attracted to Omovo partly because of his sensitivity, and partly because his oddity makes him stand out. (She is the only person around, for example, who appreciates his unusual hairdo.) The growing bond between them is not, however, strong enough to prevent her eventually running away to her village, where she is casually murdered when mistaken for somebody else.

In *Landscapes Within* the somewhat fragmentary and undeveloped account of Ifi's and Omovo's amours reads too much like added romantic interest to be entirely convincing. By the time Okri came to revise the story as *Dangerous Love*, he had come to see this strand as a major element to the story, as the new title implies. Yet already in the first version there is much that is instructive about this painful entanglement, above all in the parity between Omovo's attitude towards it and the implied attitude adopted by the narrative voice. Both regard it with suspended judgement. In Omovo's case, this is because his sympathy for, and attraction towards, Ifi dwarf all other considerations. Is he, we wonder with relevant persistence, irresponsible in what he does? In the narrator's case, tolerance is impelled by a recognition of at least two of the parties – Ifi and Takpo – as victims. Admittedly Takpo is a truly brutish husband: overbearing, violent, and coarse. Yet the most moving scene in the book is that in which this seeming ogre takes his bewildered young spouse to the bush, and begs her to show him love and respect (*LW* 232–5; *DL* 231–6). There is an unflinching authenticity about this moment that enables us to see Takpo as tragic, and that mitigates even Ifi's dismay and disgust with something approaching pity. When all are so damaged, what place is there for indictment or moralizing of any kind?

The book achieves this even stance through the honesty with which events are recounted, a candour that mirrors Omovo's own attentiveness. One of the recurrent epithets in the narrative is 'clear'. When Omovo looks at the houses of Alaba in the morning light, 'all were clear to him', 'His mind was clear' (*LW* 114). When Omovo and Okocha part company after a meeting of minds, 'The road was clear. Everything was clear' (*LW* 30). In Omovo's painting of a traffic jam, 'People were walking in the background and foreground – and they were very clear' (*LW* 155). When he executes four swift miniatures of a boy's face, 'The drawings were beautiful and clear and sensitively shaded' (*LW* 165). As he observes the to-ings and fro-ings at the chemicals factory where he works, 'everything became clear and definite and clear-cut' (*LW* 193). In the last resort, it is this very lucidity that proves threatening.

Another recurrent term is 'silence'. Time and time again in the book, busy or halting conversations peter out into wordless transcendence. When Omovo and Ifi first make love, 'The silence between them was like a presence' (*LW* 211). The erotic hush is momentarily interrupted by a cloud of mosquitoes, droning 'like small badly tuned pocket transistor radios'. Afterwards they get dressed 'in a different kind of silence' (*LW* 215). Pauses such as these are so much more highly charged than the book's occasionally prosaic dialogue that they carry much of the meaning.

The Landscapes Within is a book that reflects what one might call the subversiveness of reticence. Society disapproves of

Omovo because he is quiet and paints what he sees. The narrative of the novel too is quiet in its overall manner. It too relates what it observes. In so far as the work has a message, that is it: the menace – and the sustained responsibility – of such self-contained, undemonstrative watchfulness.

These concerns were to remain with Okri, and inform his later work. To some extent they remain integral to his thinking. In the second part of 'The Joys of Storytelling', he turns to consider the potential implicit in all narratives for 'transgression'. His suggestion – the cumulative result of two decades at unemphatic odds with the social and political status quo – is that the resistance to the way the world offered by fiction as against more direct forms of social action frequently takes the form, not of a statement, but of mild interrogation. Indeed the writer is sometimes most subversive when his enquiry does not even proceed as far as an implied question mark. Self-standing loveliness can be just as effective in its mute indictment of brutality: 'Transgression', writes Okri, 'can also reside in creating a beautiful thing. Sometimes the creation of a beautiful thing in a broken resentful age can be an affront to the living, a denial of suffering. Sometimes beauty can be accusatory' (WBF 65). It is just this sort of composed and intelligent query in the face of chaos and corruption that the young Okri offers us in his first two novels.

4

The Visible City, 1978–1991

I am ashamed to admit it, but I hate suffering.

Stars of the New Curfew

It is the cause, it is the cause, my soul.

(*Othello*, IV. ii. 1)

Okri had been drawn to London by the reputation of what the Bengali writer Nirad C. Chaudhuri – a literary pilgrim of a much earlier generation – once called the 'Platonic England' of its great books. 'I went to London because, for me, it was the home of literature', he confided fourteen years later. 'I went there because of Dickens and Shakespeare. No, let's say Shakespeare and Dickens, to get them in the right order.'[1] He also had dim recollections of a happy childhood spent among the neglect and grime of south London, but the reality proved a shock. Admiring Shakespeare, he soon found himself living through one of his more exacting plays. The only contact address that he possessed was that of a distant uncle, a recurrent law student, in New Cross, about three miles from the Peckham of his remote early boyhood. He probably did not realize at the time that Dickens had once lived in New Cross. In any case, the district he was making for had been partially flattened by German bombs during the Second World War. The planners were completing the destruction:

> When I asked the way to New Cross, people walked away. I was shocked. I had always thought the English were friendly. When I got to my uncle's street, it was as if I hadn't travelled. The houses were boarded up. There were hundreds of rats. I was given a funny room with a broken window through which came the bright yellow light of a street-lamp. It was Nigeria in London I thought.[2]

Unpleasant as it was, this exposure to the less salubrious areas of Britain's metropolis – neglected, run-down, indigent – was fortunate for Okri's art. Through it he was to rediscover an important theme: the imaginative redemption of deprivation. When Christmas time came round, no unreformed Scrooge could have wished this young author a more forlorn one, set amid sickness and sorrow:

> My uncle's illness, which was later to lead to his death, over-shadowed the period. The children had tasted deeply of desolation before they had even entered their adolescence. The house was very decrepit and cold. We were the only ones left in the street, which was full of rubbish and in which only one lamp functioned. When we looked out of the window we saw only impersonal tower blocks in the mist.[3]

'There are some parts of London which are necessary', wrote Iris Murdoch in her first novel *Under the Net*, 'and others which are contingent'.[4] New Cross is contingent – off the cultural map. For that very reason it is a fertile field for fiction, though at first Okri knew this imperfectly. He moved out to a bedsit in Plumstead – a district almost as contingent, yet not quite as poor. One fortunate result of his stay in New Cross, however, had been the physical proximity of Goldsmiths College, a constituent part of London University with a long tradition of providing part-time education for adults, where he took evening classes in Afro-Caribbean literature over that severe winter. (In January 1979, the snow was so deep over much of south London that the traffic ground to a halt for several days.)

For a while, his circumstances improved. At the suggestion of his Goldsmiths tutor Jane Grant, he sent *Flowers and Shadows* off to the firm of Longman, for whom her husband wrote textbooks. They accepted it for publication in July 1980 in their 'Drumbeat' series, which had been launched in the summer of 1979 as a showcase for recent African writing. He won a place at the University of Essex to read Literature, and a Nigerian government scholarship that enabled him to accept it. By the time he reached university, the novel had appeared, so that, in student circles at least, he was something of a celebrity. He was soon to learn how hollow a consolation is mere renown. At Christmas virtually all of the British students, including his girlfriend, went home to their families. Once more, he was alone:

> The only students left on the campus were some Chinese students, who kept to themselves, and some rebellious undergraduates who had become alienated from their family. There was an anarchist, two communists, a Spanish existentialist and a Christian. I think it was the existentialist who invited the rest of us up to spend Christmas together. It was an evening of unfathomable gloom. Our conversation seemed to dwell exclusively on suicide that night. Then the Christian talked about Christ. Then the anarchist said, with astounding confidence, that God was dead. A hush fell on us.[5]

Returning to his room across the cold and deserted Wivenhoe Park campus, he thought of the closing moments of James Joyce's story 'The Dead', where the disconsolate protagonist Michael Furey stands at a window observing snow settling over a forlorn Dublin churchyard: 'His soul swooned slowly as he heard the snow falling faintly through the universe and faintly falling, like the descent of their last end, upon all the living and all the dead.'[6]

During his second year, Okri's grant was withdrawn by the cost-cutting government of President Shehu Shagari. He moved back to London, where he worked as a freelance journalist whilst composing shorter works of fiction towards an eventual volume. Eventually he began presenting the BBC African Service's regular magazine programme *Network Africa* at what was the princely sum of £50 per transmission. On my resignation in 1983 he also took over the position of Poetry Editor for the then flourishing weekly magazine *West Africa*, whose offices were situated in Holborn Viaduct on the fringes of the City (they were later to move to the Gray's Inn Road and subsequently, during the journal's declining years, to Brixton). Scrupulosity marked all that he did: editorial eyebrows were raised at the magazine, for instance, by his refusal to print all but the best poetry. In conversation, or even in one's thoughts, his principal characteristic seemed to be an affectionate play-fulness beneath which surged a revolutionary – though always ceremonious – ardour. One or two jottings in my journals convey this impression. One recounts the mocking conclusion to an argument over some matter of literary taste. It runs: 'Ben to me (*with an incisive gesture of the right hand*): "You are *revoked*!" '[7] Another refers to his insistence that women should always be treated with proper courtesy rather than with the cavalier insouciance of which I was then occasionally guilty. It records that 'Ben told me off the other day for talking about "birds", said this had much relevance to the way that I regard people.'[8] There was always an element of self-deprecating humour behind these gentle rebukes.

Some more trenchant insights into Okri's state of mind over these years are afforded by a series of articles that he wrote at the time for the left-wing periodical the *New Statesman* about the position of a minority artist in a metropolitan and pluralist society. Many of these pieces centre on the issue of race, a concern that in the years since Okri has tended to subsume into a larger, universalist argument. His journalistic vignette about arriving footsore from Nigeria in London belongs to this category, as do his downbeat descriptions of not-quite-Dickensian Christmases. Even more noteworthy is an account in the 'Backchat' column on 17 October 1986 of a concert that he had recently attended given by the 22-year-old jazz saxophonist Courtney Pine. It is a remarkable piece of writing, as subtle in its way as Pine's music. Okri had called in at the venue by chance and introduces his experience there as a piece of sublime luck, a pure gift of grace. 'When they say that a stream of invisible forces flows to make the unexpected,' he begins, 'I confess that, in spite of my own protective cynicism, I have to believe it.' After a description of Pine's playing, compared to 'the mirrors of angels that Rilke talked about', he opens into a candid peroration. Courtney Pine is a relatively young man and, confesses Okri, 'I fear for him':

> With the black individual in the West, talent is always political. The gifted individual becomes one of the focal points of the conflicting yearnings, frustrations, historical pains and misapprehensions of the people who are aware of them. And the individual is too small a frame to take all of that projection. That is perhaps why unusual ability always carries with it a tremendous sadness, a definite fatalism. Lights from the mirrors of angels converge on them in fragile beams: the world converges on them with the hardness of an unbearable hunger. From all that multiplication,

that individual's distorted reflections appearing in unlikely places, there could be fragmentation on the one hand, silence on the other.'[9]

Various strands come together in this account. There is Okri's metaphysical delight in the serendipities of circumstance and talent, both of which he explicitly compares to the unseen though palpable operations of Rilke's angels. This, however, is intertwined with an argument about visibility and invisibility that was to run right through Okri's fiction, criticism, and poetry. With time and increasing maturity it was to gather to itself all kinds of permutations and meanings: social, political, aesthetic, even religious. It begins here with Pine centre stage surrounded by admirers alert to his talent but blind to him as a man. At this point, where artistic pre-eminence and social occlusion meet and cancel one another out, a complex and ramifying dialectic is born.

Initially, as here, it corresponds to a law of inverse proportion and runs like this. A stranger in any society – be he black, white, or green – is on show for much of the time, since people habitually notice his difference. Yet in another deeper sense – the sense employed, for example, by Ralph Ellison's classic novel of American race relations *Invisible Man* – nobody sees him.[10] He is unwanted, his complex emotional and mental life of minimal account. By the same token, if this individual possesses a marked talent – for music, say, or literature – the public at large, the gawping, appreciative public, observe its effects, and may even pay him homage through hero worship. This very adulation, however, prevents the public from perceiving what has produced these remarkable effects in the first place: in Rilkean language, the light shards from angelic mirrors, in plainer speech, the unseen operations of skill or of art. His own recourse, his ultimate revenge, is his confident reliance on these unseen, sustaining forces. It goes without saying that in this piece, published just a couple of months after the appearance of the collection *Incidents at the Shrine*, where his own authentic and unmistakable voice is clearly heard for the first time, Okri is speaking – if only to a minor extent – about himself.

These observations are amplified in an article that Okri wrote for *West Africa* three years later, after watching the

half-Indian British actor Ben Kingsley (Krishna Bhanji) interpret the role of Othello for the Royal Shakespeare Company.[11]
'Leaping out of Shakespeare's Terror' takes the form of a series
of linked meditations on the themes of otherness and same-
ness, failure and success, visibility and invisibility. It is a piece
about the difficulties of living as a marked man in a shifting
and critical society, but it also concerns the ambivalent
Coleridgean quality of empathy as seen on the stage of a
theatre, in the auditorium, and in the city streets beyond. Okri
begins by spotlighting himself as a member of the audience at
the Barbican Theatre. There he sits, acutely aware of the one
visible factor that connects him with the protagonist of
Shakespeare's tragedy, but that also separates him from the
actor taking that role, from the remainder of the cast, and – in
embarrassed imitation of the circumstances up on stage – from
most of the audience. 'My skin glowed,' he remembers in a
rare autobiographical aside. 'I felt illuminated, unable to hide'
(*WBF* 71).

This, in the play, is the 'chromatic tension' that Skakes-
peare's main character feels, though Othello has been forced to
repress that awareness so as to rise in the military hierarchy of
Venice. Othello is like Courtney Pine with a sword rather than
a saxophone. He is surrounded by sycophants and by enemies,
the most intelligent among whom is Iago. Iago is able to
destroy him because he understands only too well the force of
humiliation that binds him down, the jealousy and envy that
he feels. Then in a masterstroke Okri implies what few of the
play's other critics have ever appreciated. It is Iago who
experiences sexual jealousy as much as – if not more than – his
commander-in-chief: 'Any black man who has gone out with a
white woman knows that there are a lot of Iagos around' (*WBF*
80). Othello himself is far more concerned about the problem
of whom amongst his apparently loyal colleagues he can trust.
This is only one of a number of parallels that the essay draws
between the world of the play and the alternative politics of
1980s Britain. In contemporary circumstances, Okri argues,
Othello would have become not a political radical but a highly
competitive careerist (in the Thatcher years he would most
likely have sat on the board of a merchant bank). Correspond-
ingly, Iago would never have sunk so low as to join the

National Front; he is not that crass. In the modern world he might well have masqueraded as a fervent, pamphlet-touting, anti-racist. It is our recognition of the hollowness of Iago's apparent sympathy, and of his victim's unawareness of that hollowness, that makes Othello's isolation so terrible. The final twist is that Iago has a close, though unacknowledged, imaginary affinity with Othello, whom he really hates because he reflects certain alien, unintegrated parts of himself. In any age, race prejudice is largely composed of such perverse subconscious transference: 'The other is ourselves as the stranger' (*WBF* 87).

For the Othellos of 1980s Britain, life was made still more difficult by one fact. In an effort to control crime, the Metropolitan Police had recently revived certain vagrancy laws enacted by Lord Liverpool's administration in 1824 to vet the behaviour of soldiers returning from the Napoleonic Wars. The reactivated 'sus' laws, as they became known, permitted constables to apprehend any citizen loitering with apparent intent to steal. In practice, this legitimized a police officer stopping anyone who, in his opinion (in the 1980s, it was usually 'his'), was behaving suspiciously. The provision was liberally interpreted. A friend of mine, a theologically inclined medievalist, was apprehended one night for the offence of thinking about St Augustine under a street lamp. About this time I was questioned for taking an unhealthy interest in the Rococo architecture of Hampstead Parish Church. If you were from Nigeria, you did not have to be *doing* anything.

The provisions, which led to the Brixton riots of 1981, were gradually phased out by Mrs Thatcher's Tory government. They had already caused havoc in race relations. Of arrests made under the laws in 1975, 42 per cent were of black people, who at the time constituted 4 per cent of the population. No sooner were these powers withdrawn than they were replaced in 1984 by fresh provisions authorizing police officers to 'stop and search' citizens on sight. *Plus ça change, plus c'est la même chose.*

In the *New Statesman* in March 1985 Okri recounted a relevant occurrence in his own recent history. The article was called 'Labelled' and began: 'I suspect that people invent categories in order not to take you seriously.' Okri had been planning out his short story 'Disparities' set, like the incident itself, among the London streets. One night when out walking he paused under a lamp to scribble a note. Out of the corner of his eye he noticed a pair of police constables slowly approaching. After asking for his identity card, they searched him, and one of them found the incriminating notebook. He read it without comprehension, and then asked Okri what he did for a living. Okri answered that he was a writer:

> 'YOU WRITE?' He said incredulously.
> 'Yes.'
> 'YOU WRITE?' he said, again.
> 'Yes.'
> 'What do you write?'
> 'Stories.'
> 'Love and things like that?'
> I nodded, for reasons of complicity. There was a long silence as both these perfectly literate specimens of the British police force stared at me.
> 'You must be the only one who reads them,' said one of the policemen, who then burst out laughing. He thought it perfectly funny.
> 'Published anything?' the other one said.
> 'Two books.'
> Another long silence. I had really committed a crime. Their faces turned sour.
> 'Did you say TWO BOOKS?'
> 'Yes.'[12]

'Labelled' is not so much about injustice as about perception, or what Okri was to call in his Othello piece appearance and reality. In the eyes of these officers of the law, presented I think less as authority figures than as average citizens, a black author – still more a doubly published black author – was an anomaly. Nothing in their experience had prepared them for meeting one of these living contradictions on the beat. In this they were typical of the community as a whole, whose awareness of literary values is, let us face it, fairly limited. If such false perceptions were confined to the constabulary, they would have been sufficiently troubling. Unfortunately, they were, and are, a lot more pervasive. Okri introduces this incident by recounting an equally baffling – and in its own way demoralizing – encounter: his attempts when first entering the field of literary hackwork in London in the early 1980s to attract reviewing commissions. To his dismay he found that the typical literary editor of that date assumed that Afro-Caribbean writers would be interesting only in covering books by other Afro-Caribbean authors. The possibility that such potential contributors might be interested in literature as such did not seem to occur to him. This in turn is presented as an aspect of an even wider problem: the background of expectation against which such authors were and are read. When it comes to the appreciation of Afro-Caribbean literature, publishers and readers are seldom colour-blind. As a black author, 'If you are not published because of your colour, you are read because of it.' This predisposition itself reflects that labelling or 'naming' tendency in society at large whose semantic structure I have already discussed. Its recognition rapidly came to affect Okri's understanding of the relationship between literature and meaning, meaning and society. It also helps explain why from the late 1980s onwards he steered clear of publishing outlets such as the Longman 'Drumbeat' Series set aside for minority authors, and made instead for mainstream lists where he hoped – sanguinely perhaps – that he might enjoy more freedom.

A meeting with an extraordinary fellow writer in the very early 1980s can only have reinforced some of these lessons. In February 1978 there had arrived in London a dishevelled literary genius called Dambudzo Marechera.[13] After quitting Zimbabwe in a cloud of political scandal, Marechera had won a scholarship to New College, Oxford, which he had been obliged to leave after attempting to burn it to the ground. He had then spent several weeks living in a tent on the banks of the river Isis hammering out on a portable typewriter a masterpiece called *House of Hunger*, describing in fictional terms his tribulations in Rusape township where he had grown up. When Heinemann Educational Books accepted the book for their African Writers' Series, Marechera had gravitated to the capital, where his cachet increased when in November 1979 *House of Hunger* was made joint-winner of the Guardian Fiction Prize. Arriving at the ceremony wearing a kaftan and poncho and clutching a copy of the *Cantos* of Ezra Pound, he had proceeded to hurl glasses at the guests. In 1981, when Okri met him whilst still studying at Essex, Marechera was intermittently living in a communal squat near King's Cross or, when he failed to find a roof, sleeping on benches in London Parks. There he too inevitably became an object of curiosity to the police. Okri himself experienced spells of homelessness during these years. For Marechera, the lack of a roof over his head was a quasi-permanent – indeed almost a defining – condition.

It is difficult to assess what was most remarkable about Marechera: the voracity of his reading across a range of European and African literatures; the prolixity of his conversation as – night after night and surrounded by Desdemonas – he held court in the downstairs bar at the African Centre, Covent Garden; the precocious torrent of his writing.[14] Despite the halting handicap of a speech impediment, which he conquered with an egregious Oxford accent, he would expatiate with skill and assurance on a remarkable number of subjects, holding as he did so many people – Okri included – in his thrall. He was daring; he drew you out. As for his fluency at writing, it was not so much celebrated as notorious. One night when Okri had given him hospitality after closing time at the Africa Centre, Marechera began to compose a play on his portable. Okri soon fell asleep. When he awoke, he found that his guest had completed the three-act work, the closely typed manuscript of which rested beside him. Dambudzo would bring off feats of this order, time after daunting time. Though much of the resulting work required revision, there was no stopping him: the supply of rough-and-ready (but always vigorous and lively) first drafts seemed endless.

In February 1982 Marechera was lured back to Zimbabwe to work on an abortive television project. He never returned to Britain. In Harare as in London his social existence was that of a vagrant. Despite the appearance of a second book, *Black Sunlight*, in 1981, he gradually acquired an aura of unpublishability. He was perhaps the most impressive example of raw talent that any of us had ever known, but he was also the most distressed example of just those pressures on the individual black artist that Okri was to analyse with such insight in his journalism of the mid-1980s. The problem was that Marechera had no game plan to deal with these burdens apart from internalizing them and, overtly, of living and writing out a charade in which the false perceptions of society were projected back in stylish, clowning parody. As an artist, he was *sans pareil*; as a role model, unpromising.

In my notebook for January 1987 I find the following sketch for a story that may have owed something to my reading of Saul Bellow's novel *Humboldt's Gift*, but that also alluded to my immediate social *milieu*. It consisted of 'two components':

1. A young author setting out in the world with much seemingly against him, and little to call his own apart from his remarkable talent. Before him beckons an all-encompassing chaos. He is forewarned by the example of:
2. Another author, a few years his senior who, destroyed by the pressures of an unsympathetic society, has resigned control over his life, is the butt of jokes and the prey of policemen, sleeping rough, abusing even the hospitality of his friends, dishevelled, disorganised, with finally even his talent in tatters.[15]

As I see the matter now, I had no need to write that story. It is more or less what happened.

Eight months later, in August 1987, shortly after my family and I had moved house, Okri phoned me. A few days previously, Damdudzo had died from pneumonia in a Harare Hospital.[16] His ghost still hangs around the edges of conversations: mocking, provoking, goading. There is something about his memory and example that even now inhabits hesitations and permeates judgements, even the difficult ones of Shakespearian interpretation. In September 2000 Okri went to the Lyttleton, the National Theatre's proscenium auditorium, to see John Caird's production of *Hamlet* with Simon Russell Beale in the title role. Afterwards in a restaurant he posed a seemingly straightforward question: 'What is Hamlet *doing*?' I tried a number of suggestions: delaying killing the king, playing false to Ophelia, pondering the meaning of existence. 'No' replied Okri with slow emphasis. 'Hamlet is surviving.'

5

Microcosms: Fictions, 1982–1988

> They shoot people who can't speak their language.
>> (Ben Okri, 'Laughter beneath the Bridge')

> And makes one little roome, an every where.
>> (John Donne, 'The Good-Morrow')

Gradually Okri acquired a habit of imaginative transfusion that enabled him to realize the confusion and beauty of one city through the tribulations and splendours of another. London became Lagos, and Lagos London. The bleak campus of Essex University in a snowfall was transformed in his mind into the Dublin of Joyce's short stories. This habit of mind gave him back his art, dressed with new assurance. The short story – and the example of Joyce in particular – provided a model of construction and inner tension.[1] It also conveyed a valuable lesson: if you want to build *Ulysses* or *Finnegans Wake*, start small.

Accordingly, Okri devoted most of the mid-1980s to shorter fictional forms. The two volumes of stories that resulted – *Incidents at the Shrine* (1986) and *Stars of the New Curfew* (1988) – show him grappling with a number of influences, and growing in a variety of directions. Stylistically, these collections possess a purity and concentration far in excess of that displayed in his apprentice novels. Both interestingly carry epigraphs from Okri's spiritual guide, Christopher Okigbo. All of these tales, moreover, show him reassessing, and expanding upon, a mechanistic model of human probability. In the process they prepare the way for the innovative and professionally successful novel sequence that came next.

The variety of technique in *Incidents at the Shrine* is already remarkable. Two of these 'compacted narratives' (*WBF* 68),

'Laughter beneath the Bridge' and 'Crooked Prayer', are related by a child who only half understands what he has witnessed. The effect in both cases lies in the contrast between the reader's assumed level of awareness and the narrator's. Another pair of stories – 'Disparities' and 'Converging City' – encourage the reader's inner eye to wander at will over a dispersed townscape – in the first case in London, in the second in Lagos – following up arbitrary and fortuitous connections. 'Masquerades' constitutes a mini-exercise in mystery and menace. 'A Hidden History' and the title story 'Incidents at the Shrine', though very different in other respects, are both almost parabolic in their approach to meaning, whilst the longest and last tale – 'A Dream Vendor's August' – is constructed almost like an Aesop fable.

Two of the pieces are situated in London, five in Lagos, and one in an unspecified location in rural Nigeria. All of the environments described are projections of a turbulent yet controlled artistic vision. These stories stare ugliness in the face, transmuting it in the process into something rich and strange. It is as if Omovo has transferred his attentions to fiction.

'Laughter beneath the Bridge', set in the hinterland of the Nigerian creeks during the early months of the Civil War, has a complicated semantic and philosophical structure dependent on the relative ignorance of its unnamed young protagonist. Its readers must travel through a reassessment of the characters, of themselves, of war, and of social tragedy in general. To begin with, the 10-year-old narrator regards the unrest around him – especially the disruptions in the school timetable – as fun. This may seem a terrible misreading of national events. The terrible fact is that it is a psychologically authentic one. As all that have lived through armed conflict can testify, war conveys a number of different impressions. Amongst them, it features as a collective and individual diversion. The story examines this paradox, what we can learn from it, and how we can go beyond it to a different – though not necessarily a deeper – understanding.

'I remember it as a beautiful time,' remarks the young narrator; 'I don't know why.' He is sitting with his two remaining classmates observing the forlorn countryside around him whilst planes circle overhead (*IS* 3). The boy never quite works out the source of his appreciation, though the narrative helps us interpret it for him. War is vital: it shakes life up. It also produces a compensatory aesthetic of desolation. A fine example of this occurs in the same paragraph, when a scarecrow in the middle of a blasted field turns out to be the child's, at first unrecognized, mother.[2] The ensuing scene with her sheltering the three boys under her arms has the eloquence of a sculptural tableau by, say, Henry Moore, or a picture by an artist like Graham Sutherland. It is graphic war poetry.

Further aspects of the cruel, sometimes comic, pathos of conflict surface during the lorry journey undertaken by mother and son in search of safety. At the final checkpoint, to identify their ethnic origin and allegiance, each passenger is obliged to recite the paternoster – that manifesto for peace – in his or her mother tongue, to the accompaniment of a rape going on behind the bushes (*IS* 5–9). The mother saves her skin by mumbling the paternoster in her husband's language (presumably Urhobo) rather than her own Igbo. As the boy's turn comes, he is disabled by laughter. When the commanding officer attempts to clout him into submission, he has a vision of the *egungun* masqueraders in his home village. He is rescued from arrest and separation from his mother when he cries out the word for 'shit' in his father's tongue.

Further surprises await him in the village. His girlfriend Monica has taken to processing around the town in the company of the local *egungun* troupe. Okri manages to suggest the significance of her intrusion (traditionally *egungun*s are all male affairs), without encumbering us with literal explanation. The fact is that *egungun*s impersonate the dead. An *egungun* masquerade is a festival of mourning, celebration, and continuance. Like this story, it treads a narrow path between tragedy and joy. Monica appreciates the euphoric versatility of the rite; she is too young to be aware of its darker layers. She and the boy follow the masqueraders down to the river. They mock the soldiers on sentry-go, flirting with mortality in more than one sense, since bloated corpses fester among the bull rushes. The moment when the boy recognizes these grotesque cadavers for what they are is one of the most dramatic in the book (*IS* 17–18). Carried away by the delicious liberation of the masquerade – their saturnalian mood blending with the delirium of civil discord – the children eventually go too far. Monica confronts the sentries dressed in a mask of her own making: she is taken away. The boy learns the boundary between levity and seriousness. We, who have witnessed the fate of the woman in the bush, do not need to be told what her fate might be. In the words of the concluding sentence, a quote from the lorry's logo: 'the young shall grow' (*IS* 22).

'Laughter beneath the Bridge' forms an implied pairing with the last-but-one story 'Crooked Prayer', also narrated by a child, the mood of which is like a scherzo after a tragic overture (*IS* 91–104). The narrator's uncle is having an affair with a woman called Mary, with whom he comes to co-habit once she has given him the child his infertile wife has been unable to produce. The arrangement is facilitated by errands run in all innocence by the young narrator. Structurally the situation has something in common with the novel *The Go-Between* (1953) by the British author L. P. Hartley (1895–1972), memorably filmed in 1970 under the direction of Joseph Losey. It differs from Hartley's novel and Okri's war story, however, by enshrining a profound joke. All of the moral issues in the tale, the uncle's cavalier behaviour, his manipulation of his nephew, and his behaviour towards his spouse and his mistress, are spelled out quite clearly to the readers. The source of our information, however, is the admiring nephew, who is not in the least aware of them.

Formally speaking, both 'Laughter beneath the Bridge' and 'Crooked Prayer' owe something to Joyce: in their deliberate omissions, their ear for dialogue, their blending of sweet with sour. The truly revolutionary potential of Okri's technique, however, is even clearer in my next pairing: 'Disparities', set in south-east London, and 'Converging City', situated in a commercial district of Lagos. 'Disparities' brought Ben to the attention of the British novelist Peter Ackroyd, who published it in 1984 in the anthology *PEN New Fiction 1*, of which he was editor.[3] At the time Ackroyd was writing his giant biography of Dickens, eventually published in 1990.[4] Ten years later, he was to issue a 'biography' of London.[5] It is not hard to see what he liked about 'Disparities', a portrait of contemporary London drawn from Dickensian depths. It was arguably Okri's first contribution to British literature, a story that, like Dickens's fiction and to a lesser extent Ackroyd's, transforms the cityscape utterly.

Structurally speaking, both stories resemble a set of overlapping circles. 'Disparities' situates its bemused if alert protagonist – a black, though not a Nigerian, vagrant – at the point of convergence.[6] His is a character overburdened, both by history (James Joyce again[7]) and by a morbid if inspired sensitivity. His kinship with Omovo can be gleaned from the following passage:

> Not far from where I was going to sit there was a bird. Maggots crawled out of its beak. I stared at it for a while, all sorts of temptations going through my mind. It was unturned in a grotesque enchantment and for a while I experienced a cluttered remembrance of all those fairy-tales that were bludgeoned into us when young. The memories irritated me. I spat generously and then I lay down. There seemed no distance between me and the sky. I hate skies. They seem to me a sentimental creation. (*IS* 41)

Birds, of course, are a stock-in-trade of British fairy tales and visual art. It also helps to know that representation of the sky has been one of the radical achievements of European painting, from seventeenth-century Dutchmen like Jacob van Ruisdael (1628–82) and Meindert Hobbema (1638–1709), to British artists such as J. M. W. Turner (1775–1851) and the 'Norfolk School' of watercolourists. So successful had these painters been in reinterpreting and revisualizing clouds, for example, that by the late twentieth century it had become impossible to admire a patch of sky or a sunset without thinking of them as 'picturesque'. In this passage Okri has taken these now-hackneyed perceptions apart. There is even something of the dash of an avant-garde painter in his portrayal of that maggot-ridden bird, an iconoclastic zeal worthy of the Turner-prize-winning British artist and specialist in animal corpses, Damien Hirst (b. 1965). As for the sky depicted, it is simply banal. Okri's vagrant, moreover, seems quite conscious of the revolutionary nature of his insights, and the paradoxes he has formulated to express them. In effect, he is a latterday Wildean figure: the Tramp as Critic.

This character – jaundiced, but oddly attractive in his disillusionment – wanders from street to street, rewriting, repainting the city as he goes. At one point he strays into a student squat (*IS* 38–40). Its ludicrous inhabitants owe something to Okri's own Essex experience, but they also suggest the worlds of the cult British movie *Withnail and I*, which depicts the squalid living conditions of out-of-work actors, and of the 1980s television sitcom *The Young Ones*, set in a student flat-share. In a Muriel Spark-like pub he then encounters a garrulous pensioner whose woes assume a quality of surreal epic (*IS* 45–8). The lower the narrator sinks, the higher his artistry flies. He is most buoyant when relying on the simplest of means. The most satisfying sentence in the story – a Chekovian near tautology – describes the student squat: 'The room had been cleared up, it was almost – a room' (*IS* 39).

The companion story, 'Converging City' – initially entitled 'Lagos Blues'[8] – has much the same overlapping structure, except that it employs third-person narrative (*IS* 23–36). It combines that technique with something more radical: an experiment in relative velocities. The trader J. J. Agodi's ruin speeds up, threatening to spin out of control. As it accelerates, a tension is evident between the centrifugal vortex of circumstance and the centripetal efforts of Agodi's will-power. In the end, he loses everything, but, in a manner by now typical of Okri, he plucks spiritual victory out of the jaws of economic defeat. One of Okri's 'tangential narratives' (*WBF* 68), the story is as full of oblique possibilities and of ambiguous identities as any work by, say, Wilkie Collins. Unlike Collins, it offers no solutions to its varied mysteries. Instead, there are pointers to interpretative possibilities. Agodi belongs to the Church of Eternal Hope; the hope at the end of the story is seemingly just as evanescent. Ajasco Atlas, the dwarf and strongman who plays a prominent role in the ongoing farce, could well be in league with Agodi's impatient and devious landlords. A customer in tatty underpants enters his lean-to shack of a shop. Agodi suspects him of being a thief. The stranger flees and collapses in the middle of the road, causing a traffic jam during which the military Head of State is almost assassinated in his limousine. We are left to wonder whether the whole episode has been staged as an ambush. But we cannot fail to notice that an attempted assassination, a major political event after all, has been relegated to the sidelines. More Damien Hirst-like spectacles occur in the shape of dead animals: a lizard and, more explosively, a festering cow. So skilful and deliberate are these effects that the story seems to have been written by a writerly equivalent of Omovo. Craft steals the limelight from politics. The *generalissimo*, meanwhile, has a walk-on – or rather drive-in – part.

'Masquerades'(*IS* 67–80) is among the more artificial items in the book: an exercise in menace and mystery that recalls Graham Greene or perhaps Harold Pinter. Who is this oddball who haunts hotel bars importuning prostitutes, and who are the sinister figures hanging about outside his house? He is sympathetically drawn and yet socially inadequate; the decor of his home also suggests he is a fantasist. At the end of the story we discover that he is a night-soil worker, but this Pinteresque attribution is complicated by our suspicion that he is being employed not by the city council but by a political group that punishes its opponents by depositing foul-smelling waste on their doorsteps. An accompanying extortion racket is also implied. The man has his comeuppance when his meticulously furnished apartment is soiled in an act of vengeance carried out, we suspect, by some vigilantes who have been watching him all along. The treatment of these themes is slightly mannered, even derivative, though Okri adds an individual touch by suggesting another side to the central vendetta. The protagonist's home has a beautiful interior as far removed as possible from the foetid atmosphere of his trade. He is notably, almost psychotically, hygiene conscious. In the end, the filth breaks through. As in *The Landscapes Within*, the barrier between beauty and ugliness is breached, and in the most dramatic of ways.

Violence and the interrogation of aesthetic categories are taken to extremes in 'A Hidden History' (*IS* 81–90). Chronologically speaking, this experimental piece is contemporaneous with Okri's articles of the 1980s about race and otherness, and initially it appeared like them in the *New Stateman*.[9] Many consider it Okri's most challenging attempt to portray the realities of modern London. It is his anti-tribute to New Cross, set in that urban no man's land that once stretched southwards from the Thames across Bermondsey and out towards Peckham. It translates this period scene into a veritable nightmare, inhabited by migrants, weirdos, and thugs. Its vigour lies in its experimentation with grammatical person.[10] Although a first-person-singular narrator is implied, the real focus of the piece is the migrant community, whose arrival, degradation, and persecution are rendered in the grammatical plural. This singularity-within-diversity, individuality-within-community, has a great liberating effect on the artistry of this tale. There is a sense of the environment as an energetic if pestiferous organic growth, as if the entire *milieu* and those who inhabit it have been converted into some burgeoning weed or plant. At the very end, the streets are puréed into an evil-looking though perversely appealing broth, like the lake of slime that so attracts Omovo in *The Landscapes Within*. It is a radical effect, as disorienting to our sense of social and artistic priorities as anything in the contemporary visual arts, for example. The tale is noticeably inscrutable – for example, in the figure of the 'listmaker', who drifts in and out, tormented by the local skinheads in much the same way as a dog in one of Okri's early novels. His status is unclear, since he is both arbiter and victim; so is his relationship to the solipcistic narrator. The tale is a tour de force. A sentence occurs to me from 'The Joys of Storytelling': 'The higher the artist, the fewer the gestures' (*WBF* 124). 'A Hidden History' is a superbly gestural piece.

'Incidents at the Shrine' (*IS* 53–66) gives the volume its title, but is almost unique within it. Its closest affinity in Okri's fiction is to the piece in the next collection called 'Worlds that Flourish' (*SNC* 83–146). Like that, it is a parable of initiation into something known but forgotten. Anderson, the main character, is an employee in the Department of Antiquities in the capital city who is paid to know about the past. In fact, he has very little sense of the history of his own people, or has chosen to suppress it. When relieved of his job, he flees back to his village of origin, where he undergoes a hermetic rite: a meeting with an Image-maker, an encounter with the Image itself, and a skirmish with 'Image-eaters', spirit-like figures on the margins of the community. The first two of these experiences are clearly rites of passage, the third what anthropologists, and some modern critics, call a 'liminal' rite – that is, a crossover between worlds.[11] The story is about zones, and the activities and insights proper to city and village. Anderson is an urban official who will work vigorously in his allotted sphere only if he retains spiritual contact with his origins; as the Image-maker tells him, 'This is where you derive power' (*IS* 64). This is the first appearance in Okri's work of a phenomenon that was to recur over and over: an esoteric process enshrining a long familiar truth.

We now enter territory that readers of Okri's later work will instantly recognize. The story in the collection that seals this new tendency is the last and longest; some readers believe it to be the best. 'The Dream Vendor's August' (*IS* 105–34) is a story about black and white magic, accident, chance, and destiny, set during West Africa's torrential rainy season. It is whimsical; it is also profound. Ajegunle Joe is a personable charlatan who makes his living by selling quack cures by post, along with pamphlets entitled 'How to Sleep Soundly' or 'How to Banish Poverty from your Life'. There is a well-established history of such self-help remedies in Nigeria; the booklets outlining them originated in Onitscha in the east but are now widespread. Despite his self-advertised expertise, Joe leads an indigent and celibate existence in one Lagos room, which is constantly being flooded. His lack of financial and personal success is rubbed in by occasional visits from his closest male friend (he has no close female associates), a charming spiv called Cata-cata. Cata is as feline, stealthy, and two-timing as his name suggests. At the beginning of the story he bribes Joe into lending him his room so that he can enjoy sex illicitly with a Ghanaian woman he has picked up, away from the prying eyes of his girlfriend. Joe obligingly makes himself scarce. He returns and falls asleep on his bed, dreaming of a 'midget with a large head and red eyes' who gives him a gift; it is called 'wisdom'. Later he falls in with the Ghanaian woman, but when they attempt to make love, he finds that he is impotent. Humiliated, he seeks various cures. At the end of the story – and the book – he goes fishing with his friend, falls asleep and sees the midget again. He asks what his present really was: '"Bad luck," the midget said, cheerfully' (*IS* 135).

The midget is Joe's other self. He is macabre yet sprightly, small but powerful, scorned and yet wise. He seems almost like a character out of a story by Daphne du Maurier, but he also epitomizes much that Okri wishes to convey, both about Joe and about magic. His gift is double-edged; it temporarily ruins Joe's already risible sex life and his slender grasp on reality. But it also gives him back his self-respect when he realizes how little it was that he was granted, how little he has lost, and how little has been restored. At the end Joe is blithe, as happy as he has ever been, happy even in the presence of the sly Cata-cata. This happiness is akin to the renunciation that Joe is careful not to preach to others. And yet that is what Joe seems to learn at the end: disinterested serenity lying in the sun on a riverbank. Like Anderson, he achieves his salvation by grasping with firmer understanding something that he already possesses. This is not a lesson likely to find favour with those who seek political answers to social ills. And yet it carries artistic conviction. It represents the most hopeful, and mildly uplifting, close to any of Okri's books up until that time.

Incidents at the Shrine is separated from Okri's next book *Stars of the New Curfew* by a gap of two years, but also by a large leap of the imagination. In the early book the influences are myriad, comparatively easy to identify, and for the most part European; in the latter they are fewer, far more intense, and largely African. Most importantly, they do not always lie on the surface of the text but inform its deeper structures. Okri was learning to keep his craft hidden from inquisitive eyes, to blend its component elements into an individual voice that would prove inimitable.

To make this point, it might be best to construe this volume story by story, but in reverse order. The last tale, 'What the Tapster Saw' (*SNC* 183–94), alludes in its title to the quick flicks that holidaymakers used to watch through coin-in-the-slot viewfinders on the promenades of British seaside resorts: 'What the Butler Saw . . .'. We expect something lurid and fun; cartoon-like and possibly titillating. Read the first paragraph, however, and you are in a different world: that of *The Palm-Wine Drinkard and his Dead Palm-Wine Tapster in the Dead's Town* by Amos Tutuola, a classic whose publication in 1952 transformed the prospects of Nigerian literature.[12] Okri had long admired Tutuola, to whom he here pays the tribute, not of imitation, but of transmutation. In the Tutuola tale, a drunkard or 'drinkard' goes in search of his tapster, who has fallen to his death while collecting palm wine from a tall tree: he eventually discovers him in the 'Dead's Town'. In Okri's reworking, the tapster himself undertakes a quest after his provisional decease. He is unaware that his life is over and, what is more, seems to have only a vague notion of the purpose of his expedition. Moreover, as the Ghanaian scholar-critic Ato Quayson remarks in the most thorough treatment this story has so far received, it is not even quite clear at what point he dies.[13]

Quayson's reading, though persuasive, is I think mistaken in certain respects. To start with, he has a literal and binary notion of the opposition between life and death. In Okri's universe, one can die several times and in different senses. Rather than there being a single 'crossover' point between the world of the living and what lies beyond – a boundary that proves difficult to locate – Okri seems to be suggesting a series of initiations into realms that lie inside one another, like the successive skins of a Russian doll. Moreover, there is no single delineation between what Quayson calls reality and what he persists in calling the 'esoteric realm'. The tapster is journeying *into* reality.

Moreover, the comic element in the story plays a larger role than Quayson allows it. Alongside references to Orphic and other epic motifs, there lingers more than a smack of Lewis Carroll's *Alice in Wonderland*, in which anything can metamorphose into anything else. The odder it appears, the truer it is on inspection. Carroll was a mathematics don. Okri too is fascinated by the unpredictable combinations revealed by, in particular, 'chaos theory' (*WBF* 102). Much that the tapster learns on his journey has this logical yet bizarre quality.

As well as being comic, the story is also political. Where Tutuola's tapster was a Yoruba, Okri's is a Urhobo; his creeks and palm groves have been taken over by the petrolium companies, who have planted notices forbidding 'drilling'. 'Drilling' implies digging down deep – precisely what the tapster is metaphorically doing. The companies have also colonized the mineral depths, corrupting its ministers and inhabitants. This is why, whenever the tapster articulates a fresh truth, one of the presiding turtles, in a Lewis Carroll-like gesture of mock admonishment, knocks him on the head. In a characteristically spry joke, Okri has also coded in a warning to literary critics. The turtles are convened in some solemn seminar 'like grave scholars without a text'. Obsessed with their own stereotyped concerns and their jargon, they have learned to ignore the evidence of their eyes.

The motif of the quest connects this story with 'When the Lights Return' (SNC 147–82), the reworking of the classical Orpheus–Eurydice myth that precedes it. Ede is a minor pop musician with one album to his name, and a pretty girlfriend called Maria. He works in one of the commercial districts of downtown Lagos – to which he, like Maria, commutes by bus – and lives with his mother in two rooms. Quayson calls him a male 'chauvinist', which is fair enough, except that a died-in-the-wool male misogynist would not suffer such agonies of remorse when his boorish behaviour towards his girlfriend drives her away. In fact Ede is a fairly average male, torn between sentimentality, vanity, and lust. The nature of his shortcomings is indicated by Maria, who draws a political parallel:

> 'I love you,' he said.
> 'That's what politicians say to the people.' (SNC 174)

Maria herself suffers from the afflictions of the good-looking: everybody wants her, and yet nobody seems to value her. After three weeks of ignoring her, Ede walks to see her in her family's bungalow in 'the infernal ghetto of Munschin', an equivalent of Hades in the Greek legend. The journey takes him across a blighted townscape, sinister and disconnected, as if the Lagos of Flowers and Shadows had been filmed by the Italian nouvelle vague director Pier Paulo Pasolini (1922–75). He arrives to find Maria dying and attended by her herbalist uncle. He walks back homewards. The lights return. Wandering into the chaotic marketplace, Ede is set upon by a hoard of indignant mammies, who slay him in a scene reminiscent of Orpheus' dismemberment by enraged Thracian women. In the last forlorn scene, his mother still awaits his return, while frogs honk futilely across the city.

Maria has earlier anticipated this death in a dream, just as he has sensed her sickness from afar (SNC 169). Telepathically, Ede and Maria inflict, or mentally will, miseries upon one another. Just before walking out on Ede during their love making, Maria predicts his neglect will kill her:

> Maria opened the car door and, with the candle-lights reflected in her eyes, said:
> 'If you do that, if you ignored me and never saw me again, then you would have killed me.'
> She looked almost demonic, almost possessed. She continued:
> 'And if you really love me, and if later you want to talk to me, you would have to wake me from death. Can you do that?'
> Ede didn't understand her. (*SNC* 152)

Ede also fails to pick up Maria's allusion to the Greek myth in this conversation. She later pointedly asks: 'do you think you are Orpheus?' (*SNC* 173). Quayson astutely observes that Ede is disqualified from embodying the master singer of legend, not simply because of lack of heroism, but also because of his mediocre musicianship. Yet, for all his faults, he is not responsible for Maria's death nor, as in the myth, does he consign her once more to Hades. Symbolically, she kills him.[14]

The longest story in the collection, and the most overtly political, is the titular 'Stars of the New Curfew', a satirical-cum-surrealist treatment of the theme of the 1970s oil boom (*SNC* 83–146). Half of it is set in Lagos; the rest in the 'Town of Scandals', 'W', an initial that fairly obviously stands for Warri, surrounded by its creeks, shallow rivers, rubber planta-tions, and ubiquitous oil concessions. Between the two wan-ders the nameless first-person narrator, a charming but hapless mountebank who bears a resemblance to Ajegunle Joe, the bogus-cures salesman of 'The Dream Vendor's August'. He blends together a tale that is further unified by its sombre view of Nigerian society in both its urban and its rural manifesta-tions, a nation dominated by an omniverous, and undis-criminating greed. Successive auctions are held. The first auction takes the form of a dream (*SNC* 92–4), in which bidders of several nations – 'the rich', comments the dreamer, 'are of one country' – compete for available lots. After outbidding one another to purchase the stars in the night sky, which go out as they are acquired, they turn their attention to the narrator, treating him as passive merchandise. The second auction takes the form of a flashback of the narrator's schooldays in the town of W, where two of his classmates – Odeh and Assi, scions of the most affluent families in town – once vied for his services as go-between with the prettiest schoolgirl in town (*SNC* 114–21). He outwits both of them, taking the girl for himself. This is followed by a reprise of the nightmare auction, in which Odeh and Assi are now the bidders, paying inflated prices for the narrator's limbs (*SNC* 123). The fourth auction, in the present-day W, takes place on the rain-soaked night of the curfew. The currency itself is the quarry (*SNC* 135–41). The money is counterfeit.

These episodes occupy a setting lit with the fitful glare of a Ben Jonson comedy. Like Jonson's London or Venice, Lagos is a grim carnival of avarice, and W is its adjunct, to which the narrator flees in an attempt to escape the human consequences of his profiteering in the city, only to find that the vices of cupidity and power are universal. In this country of oil barons, the rich compete with one another and the poor bicker for the scraps. Politics, whether national or municipal, is the expression of these drives. Takwa explains:

> 'It's all politics,' he said. 'That's what today's contest is all about.'
> 'What?'
> 'Politics,' he said.   (*SNC* 134)

The narrator is implicated in the rat race in his capacity as a drugs salesman employed by suspect firms. In his last job – to which he ruefully returns after the episode in W – he is hired to promote a phoney panacea called the POWER DRUG. His attempts to sell it aboard a crowded molue bus lead to the tragi-comic climax of the first part of the story (*SNC* 101–8), redolent of Soyinka's play *The Road*. Affected by the ill-concocted medicine, the driver loses control. Tipped from a famished road over the rickety bridge, the vehicle flops into a lagoon. 'Only' seven passengers die.

The bus, like W, is a metonym for the nation, a crowded space in which people scramble for the wherewithal to live. Okri was now acquiring the skill with synecdoche that would set him in such good stead a few years later when he came to write 'The Famished Road' sequence of novels. In the story 'In the City of Red Dust' (*SNC* 37–82) the technique is concentrated into a smaller location and duration: the eponymous city on the day of the military governor's fiftieth birthday. The tale obeys all three of the neo-classical 'unities': place (one town), time (one day), and action (one plot). It centres on two unemployed friends, Emokhai and Marjomi, who eke out an existence by picking pockets and selling blood to the Queen Mary Memorial Hospital. The 'red dust' of the title is the laterite shower that covers every surface in the city; it also alludes to the blood by which these two lost souls live. Emokhai is cool and level-headed; Marjomi hysterical and outlandish. Both are despairing, but in different keys. They are at the bottom of the economic order. Their deprivation releases in them lavish gestures, impulsive decisions, as they improvise, brilliantly, at the level of nought.

Marjomi's life is a solo routine of risk. Gambling, losing the little money he has, picking quarrels in 'bukka' bars, he falls in and out of love. He is a hopeless case, yet for him Emokhai feels an undeniable affection. In the last scene, Emokhai looks down at his friend, who is comatose after he has given his second pint of blood for the day. He admires 'the gentle ferocity of his spirit' (SNC 78). The reader has already come to discern in this broken, dissolute, and strident man something of the same quality.

Earlier that evening in the local bukka bar, Marjomi has rounded on Dede, his former girlfriend who, despite his boorish behaviour, has paid for his beer before storming out in protest. Emokhai, who has recently broken with Dede himself, invites her to his room, where he attempts, unsuccessfully, to persuade her to have sex. Later Emokhai finds out that, stalking indignantly away from his place, she has been accosted by a group of soldiers and has cut herself in the neck to avoid being molested (there is some indication that Dede has already been a victim of gang rape). She is rushed to hospital and, because she is of a rare blood group, Marjomi is taken in to give her by transfusion his second pint of the day. Personally at loggerheads, Marjomi and Dede are united by the elements that matter: common blood and equity of need. The poor shall inherit the earth. They shall also inherit one another.

'Worlds that have Flourished' is the most sophisticated piece in the book, harking back to earlier writing but anticipating developments to come (SNC 13–33). Its first-person narrator has something in common with Anderson, chief character of the title story in 'Incidents at the Shrine'. Like that story, it evokes an escape from the city to a rural location where a ritual of confrontation takes place. 'Worlds that have Flourished', however, is very much darker and more macabre than its predecessor. Okri had recently made a return visit to Nigeria, where he had observed the excesses of the military regime of General Babangida with its much-advertised 'War against Indiscipline'. This policy was intended to be a shot-in-the-arm cure for indolence and corruption; in practice it involved frogmarching suspects to jail, flogging them publicly, or subjecting them to death by firing squad. The resulting 'bar beach executions' were a popular form of entertainment at the time. The story takes this atmosphere and intensifies it to Edgar Allan Poe proportions.

Two principal vernacular influences are at work in the story, one Yoruba, one Igbo. First, like 'What the Tapster Saw', this story takes over from Tutuola's *The Palm-Wine Drinkard* the motif of a quest to the land of the dead in search of a lost self. More importantly, the title directs us to the epigraph of the book, a quotation from 'Distances', Christopher Okigbo's poetry sequence of 1962.[15] Okigbo remarked in his Preface to this extraordinary group of poems that he had been inspired by his first experience of anaesthesia; throughout the sequence surgery and unconsciousness are used as images of ordeal and sacrifice. 'Distances' plunges us into a *danse macabre* presided over by 'Death itself, the chief celebrant' seen as a murderous woman.[16] The poet is her victim, a human offering in a sacrificial rite.

'Worlds that have Flourished' adopts both of these *motifs* to which it adds concerns about names, signs, and writing. Essentially, it is an allegory of invisibility and the need to flee from limiting notions of identity. A stranger comes to the narrator in his office, and asks his name. He evades the query, dreading interference (*SNC* 13). That evening, armed robbers invade his house; apprehended by the police, they falsely identify him as their accomplice. He is imprisoned with them in foul conditions; on his release, he notices a new emptiness about the city. The face and hands of a woman to whom he speaks are 'covered in handwriting' (*SNC* 19). Making his escape by car, he drives through a thunderstorm as a lightning flash illuminates 'the handwriting on my face' (*SNC* 24). Like the woman, he seems to have been transformed into a text: 'My head', we read, 'jostled with signs' (*SNC* 21).

Roadblocks impede his excursus from the city. Arriving on foot at a village that is strange yet familiar, he learns that he is expected. A woman who – like him earlier in the story – refuses to give her name, takes him inside an *obeche* tree with a surprisingly capacious interior. (This is an international folkloristic motif, to be found in J. M. Barrie's *Peter Pan*, and also in *The Palm-Wine Drinkard*.) He escapes from the tree, and takes alarm when he hears the unseen inhabitants of this village-of-the-dead 'reciting a long list of names' (*SNC* 30). Running back along the road, he comes to consciousness in the wrecked hulk of his car. He trudges back towards the petrol station hoping to reach it 'before I died' (*SNC* 33).

We are prompted to various questions. Is the narrator alive or dead; if the second, at what juncture did he die? The ambiguity is taken over from Okigbo, but it is also present in the Tutuola story where the sprightly deceased swagger around 'Deads' Town'. Okri like Okigbo is playing with ideas about Death-in-Life and Life-in-Death such as are also present in Samuel Taylor Coleridge's poem 'The Ancient Mariner'. But in West Africa the dividing line between life and mortality is not always placed where it is in the industrialized countries of the north. As the *engungun* masquerades spell out, the ancestors are strong. The narrator is caught in a trap of conflicting classifications: not wishing to be counted among the persecuted living, but fearing being discovered in the roll call of the departed. His shiftiness of demeanour, his discomfort with names and fixed signs, betray this existential nervousness.

'In the Shadow of War', the first item in the book (*SNC* 3–12) was also the first to be written, dating from 1983, three years before the publication of *Incidents at the Shrine*.[17] Like 'Laughter beneath the Bridge', the first story in that volume, it deals with a child's experience of civil war. This time the child is our old friend Omovo, aged 7 or 8. The story stays just this side of the surreal. The woman with the black headscarf that Omovo sees and then follows, for example, could possibly be a witch, but she is just as likely to be a real-life spy magnified by a child's superstitious vision. As in so much of Okri's work, the most spine-chilling moments are those that tremble between horror and discovery, panic and rational explanation. The moment when the boy notices that 'the dead animals on the river were in fact the corpses of grown men' (*SNC* 8), for instance, is a virtual reprise of the equivalent episode in 'Laughter beneath the Bridge'. Like that tale, 'In the Shadow of War' concentrates on the moral ambiguity of military conflict. The soldiers relaxing in the bar never learn Omovo's name, since he hides behind the joking moniker 'Heclipse'. But he is just as confused about them: they slaughter the mysterious woman, but bring him home safely to his dad. We know more that he, enough in any case to be suspicious about the soldiers' motives for this piece of social work.

Taken together, these two volumes realign the standard vocabulary of *genre*. 'Short stories' does not seem the right term for them, since it suggests miniature exercises, fragments, or segments of a greater whole, like the slices of a cake. Okri's shorter fictions in contrast present us with a set of self-contained worlds, modest in physical extent, but reflecting much broader realities or universes. A useful analogy might be to the 'monads' of the German philosopher and mathematician Gottfried Leibniz (1646–1716). An alternative model is the microcosms of medieval cosmology, each representing a cosmos. Each story is like a teardrop, a pearl of dew, or that 'world in a grain of sand' of which William Blake once wrote. Like Blake, Okri had reshaped his craft with manageable accounts of innocence and experience. It was to the broader structures of a novel sequence that he turned next.

6

'When the road waits, famished', 1991–1998

> How many times is a man reborn in one life?
>
> (Ben Okri, *The Famished Road*)

> TYGER! Tyger! burning bright
> In the forests of the night ...
>
> (William Blake, *Songs of Experience*)

Okri began writing the cycle of novels called 'The Famished Road' in 1989. When published in March 1991, the first volume was largely ignored by the literary press;[1] seven months later, when it won the Booker Prize for Fiction, it was acclaimed with the hyperbole attending major literary awards. In retrospect, both the neglect and the fuss appear excessive. Indeed, the fact that the book belonged to a sequence did not become clear until the emergence of a second volume, *Songs of Enchantment*, in 1993, and the general design was not manifest until 1998 with the publication of a third, *Infinite Riches*. Moreover, despite their storylines being consecutive in time, the three books are different in kind. Over the last few years critics have wasted a lot of ink in allocating them to established literary or folkloric *genres*, or tethering them to some recognized cultural trend such as 'magic realism' or 'postmodernism'.[2] They represent something a lot more interesting: a form in the making.

Though affected by other works of the imagination, the cycle as a whole possesses a highly individual relationship to 'influence'. Take the title: both of the first book and of the sequence. The phrase 'The Famished Road' contains a half echo of a refrain in Wole Soyinka's lyrical poem, 'Death in the Dawn'. This much-anthologized elegy describes its author driving through morning mists along the then narrow – and still treacherous – road between Ibadan and Lagos in 1960. At the time of its writing Soyinka was living in Ibadan whilst directing his Independence play *A Dance of the Forests* in Lagos 100 miles to the south; he had to rise early in one city to attend rehearsals in the other. He recalls a prayer:

> The right foot for joy, the left, dread
> And the mother prayed, Child
> May you never walk
> When the road waits, famished.[3]

Here you have the elements of a situation: a mother, a child, the road with its hunger, the lurking danger of death. In the first volume of 'The Famished Road' sequence, Azaro, the boy narrator and protagonist, helps his mother to avoid the swerving peril of a truck (*FR* 9). After getting lost during a riot, he finds himself in the house with seven spectral policemen. His mother finds him, and bears him home in triumph. Later she chafes her foot against a cooking pot. She sits down murmuring 'The right foot is supposed to be lucky' (*FR* 78). Soyinka's grand premonition has turned into an informal, private moment.

Five years after composing that poem, Soyinka expanded some of its ideas into a dramatic work entitled *The Road*.[4] Characteristically mystical and satirical, it features an elusive crank named Professor who lords it over a gang of drivers and mechanics by initiating them into a death cult centred on the Lagos–Ibadan highway. Yet Soyinka's and Okri's thoroughfares are quite different. Soyinka's is a baneful and harebrained obsession. Okri's is a mode of transformation, a carriageway with an infinite number of lanes down which a boy wanders, piping enchanted songs.

He is a highly unusual child. To begin with, we never discover his real name. 'Azaro' is a nickname, a diminution of the Biblical Lazarus, described in St John's gospel being raised from the dead by Christ.[5] Azaro himself is continually resurrected, not just in that early truck-avoiding scene, but throughout the cycle, and in the special and creative sense. The Yoruba and certain contiguous groups such as the Ijọ hold that, when a mother loses several babies in succession, the same child has returned to her womb to delight and to plague her. Such 'abiku' children are both honoured and feared. At birth, rituals are performed to encourage them to stay; if they die in infancy, the corpse is scarified to discourage a reappearance (FR 4–5, 340). In the 1960s Soyinka and the Ijọ writer John Pepper Clark-Bekederimo wrote poems drawing on this custom. Clark-Bekederimo's expresses the love and apprehension of the mother,[6] Soyinka's the lofty disdain of the child.[7] 'The Famished Road' cycle voices both, and a lot more besides.

The reason for this versatility is that Okri has combined a local belief concerning child mortality both with the much broader conception of reincarnation espoused by several of the world's religions and with the remote intimations of eternal blessedness to be found in Eastern and Western literature. The doctrine of the pre-existence of the soul, for example, can be found in Plato's dialogues the *Phaedrus* and the *Apology*, while the notion that young children possess an awareness denied to adults of some prenatal bliss has a provenance reaching from the seventeenth-century mystic Thomas Traherne to Words-worth's ode 'Intimations of Immortality from Recollections of Early Childhood'. Azaro combines these attributes, both with the precocious wisdom of someone who has lived many lives and with the naivety of a 7-year-old boy. He is at one and the same time sage and innocent, possessing both a historical long view and a delighted capacity for surprise. Much critical endeavour has been expended in attempting to locate Azaro's voice. The truth is that he has many voices, and is both soloist and choir.

Azaro the soloist is located in time. He is the boisterous and affectionate only son of an impoverished couple living in one, leaky tenement room in a rural area gradually being swamped by the capital city of an African nation state on the brink of self-government. On the strictly temporal level, 'The Famished Road' sequence is one of those works of the imagination – Salman Rushdie's *Midnight's Children* might serve as another example[8] – set at the moment of independence from colonial rule. In Nigerian terms, it might be seen as taking place between late 1959 (the year of Okri's birth) and Independence

Day in October 1960. In fact, Okri is far less preoccupied with such specificities than with the cultural and human energies released by Independence as, to quote his later poem *Mental Fight* a 'Moment we have marked out|In timelessness|. . . Making a ritual, a drama, a tear|On eternity' (*MF* 3).

Accordingly, the local and temporal frame of the story is used in an almost improvisatory way. Its setting serves as a base to which the narrative reverts when not disporting itself in other, variegated, modes. There is a constant interplay between the 'present' of the narrative and a series of pasts and futures, all of which constantly enrich and feed one another. The resulting versatility extends to the mental lives of the characters, with which their enacted experience is constantly permitted to fuse, so that their dream lives constantly inform their daily doings and vice versa. As we shall see, these elisions frequently breach the walls between individual personalities and groups. The way in which they do this, however, is slightly different in each novel in the sequence, which establishes its own tempo and take on reality. Before examining Okri's technique in general, therefore, it may be wise to take a look at the performative differences between the three books.

As most commentators have noted, *The Famished Road* – the initial volume of 1991 – possesses an almost contrapuntal structure. It is like a fugue or jazz composition with two subjects: Azaro's adventures in the spirit world and his observation of, and participation in, the life of his neighourhood. Sometimes these two themes are played consecutively, sometimes simultaneously (it is a permissible Baroque or jazz technique). The idea of plotting a literary work like music comes from the clarinet-playing poet Christopher Okigbo, with whose sequence 'Distances' Azaro's successive forays are implicity linked, both thematically and verbally. Like the persona of Okigbo's poems, Azaro wanders on a series of expeditions, not *out of* reality – as some critics have thought – but *into* a world that, unseen by others, is instructively real to him. Sometimes these escapades are deliberate, as when he flees following a beating by his father (*FR* 325–9); on other occasions they are coerced, as when he is kidnapped in a sack in Madame Koto's bar (*FR* 110–12). In every case, however, his reactions fluctuate between delight at having escaped the ghetto, and relief at his eventual return. At the end of one such expedition he echoes the closing line of 'Distances': 'I was the sole witness to my homecoming' (*FR* 191).

His peregrinations establish an episodic frame, in the interstices of which the chaotic politics of Africa in the 1960s are satirically observed. In the political sphere the tone is set by the efforts of the Party of the Rich to secure a majority over the Party of the Poor in the forthcoming elections by bribing the inhabitants, notably with a dole of powdered – and, as it transpires, rancid – milk (*FR* 130–2). It is worthwhile stressing that these political arrangements bear little resemblance to Nigeria in the years 1959–60, where the three main parties were divided by region rather than by economics. Nonetheless, as there, the efforts of the power-mongers are supported by sycophants, and embarrassed by opponents and witnesses. Prominent among the aficionados of the Party of the Rich is Madame Koto, the corrupt and conniving proprietor of the local palm wine bar. Notable among the opponents is Azaro's father, Black Tyger, an amateur pugilist who earns a precarious living as a night-soil carrier and porter at the local lorry park. The witnesses include the district photographer, who insists on taking snapshots of the campaign and pasting them behind glass on a billboard in the street, and the family's next-door neighbour, a blind accordion-player, who is one of the few characters in the book to recognize Azaro as a spirit child (*FR* 321). As the conflict between these various elements intensifies, Azaro is gradually drawn into the fray. In the closing pages he resolves – for the time being at least – to remain where he is (*FR* 500).

The consequences of Azaro's decision are traced in *Songs of Enchantment*, the most earthbound of the three volumes, but paradoxically the most bizarre. Black Tyger has fallen hopelessly in love with an emissary from the world of the dead: a one-eyed girl called Helen with her gaggle of supernatural mendicants. Touched by their comely indigence, he has become an enthusiastic advocate for the Party of the Poor and for the University for Beggars that – half-literate though he is – he now intends to found. This double commitment, with its romantic undertones, enrages his wife, who stages a revolt, absenting herself from both his house and his bed. Black Tyger is driven into heroic despair. Premonitions of the political future storm the township: yellow birds, white antelopes, a jackel-headed Masquerade whose consciousness is a farrago of 'order, money, desire, power and world domination' (*SE* 115) Enraged by the growing corruption, the local carpenter collapses, hammer in hand. His spirit grips the community; anybody who buries him will be accused of his murder (*SE* 252). Black Tyger is temporarily made blind; in his delirium he determines to bury his friend (*SE* 259). The Party of the Poor makes little progress; Madame Koto grows ever more powerful and corrupt. The political stalemate, however, is compensated for by the growing awareness of the boy-soloist Azaro, who, newly devoted to the life around him, enjoys a stream of visions, not this time of the other world but of the hypothetical futures for the nation. At times this prophetic gift swells to embrace the whole community, which speaks with one voice and in the first-person plural (*SE* 154), lamenting the lost Way of the ancestors.[9] There is something brazen but pure about these intimations (at the time of writing the book, Ben spent hours listening to the music of Handel). As in a Handel opera, the people often turn into emanations of absolute, warring principles. The resulting vision appears panoptic. It is with a sense of shock that we realize in the closing bars that the whole performance has been contained within a valley, and closed off by mountains. The last paragraph of the book echoes the first; chapter one begins with the words 'WE DIDN'T SEE the seven mountains ahead of us' (*SE* 3); and the last paragraph with the sentence 'Maybe one day we will see the mountains ahead of us' (*SE* 297). Readers who wish to identify these hills may recollect the range of seven summits 'like pilings of verdigris' in the story 'Laughter beneath the Bridge' (*IS* 3).

In *Infinite Riches* the hills draw back. We are a few weeks from the threshold of independence. In his lodge the Governor General sits compiling his memoirs. In the depths of the forest, meanwhile, an elderly female recluse squats in her hut, composing an alternative account in the form of a tapestry woven from stories. Around her, teams of woodcutters despoil the ancient trees. Falsely accused of the carpenter's murder, Black Tyger is imprisoned; he is released as a result of the untiring efforts of his wife and 'the gathering wrath of women' (*IR* 20–3). Pregnant with twins, Madame Koto is planning a rally for her allies. When it arrives, it provokes a riot of symphonic proportions. Giant, ethereal presences ride through the streets. Madame Koto is assassinated by her devotees; her coffin refuses to lie still. In the aftermath of her funeral, the novel closes with a cadenza: a Rilkean poem beginning with the words 'The karmic dust of angels is everywhere . . .' (*IR* 338).

Metaphysically speaking, the sequence thus begins by positing a gulf between the world of the flesh and the world of the spirit, between which Azaro alternates and must choose. He elects for the moment to stay in the flawed but lovely land of everyday, which he interprets and conveys with the precocious insight of one who has led many lives. He cannot, however, hold ultimate truth at bay for long. In the last resort, the invisible world of the spirit barnstorms the mundane, closing the divide.

There is in this polyphonic fantasia little room for conventional characterization. A superficial reading would have it that Azaro is a spirit child isolated amongst flesh and blood mortals whom he understands with some difficulty. Look further, and *abikus* proliferate. Azaro's best friend, the epileptic Ade, virtually his only close acquaintance in his immediate generation, is also a reincarnation: he has been 'a falconer among the Aztecs' and 'a whore in Sudan' (*FR* 481). Ade narrowly avoids death during a raucous celebration towards the end of volume one (*FR* 422–3); soon afterwards Azaro sights him among the spirit children (*FR* 431); he then reappears looking fit and well (*FR* 447). He is eventually mown down by Madame Koto's driver in volume two (*SE* 195), though his presence continues to haunt the township. In the 'nation of her body' Madame Koto is herself carrying *abiku* twins (*SE* 58). Indeed, when Okri is writing at full stretch, his imagination conveys a general condition of what you might call '*abiku*hood'. Azaro, for example, describes his struggling motherland as 'an abiku-nation' that 'keeps on being reborn' after much blood and many betrayals (*FR* 494). His father, the irrepressible Black Tyger, is especially gifted with such resilience. After a bout with the ghost-boxer Yellow Jaguar, he collapses in nervous exhaustion. His neighbour, the blind accordion-player, calls at the house to serenade and revive him. When Tyger drifts back to consciousness, the musician asks him, 'How many times is a man re-born in one life?' (FR 362), a question repeated almost word for word by Ade's father, the carpenter, when his son is lying ill (FR 485).

Azaro's mother informs him that the family has regal forebears (FR 372), and Tyger himself is the grandson of the Priest of the Roads. It is not genealogy, however, that endows Azaro's father with the dignity of which he stands possessed. Dad springs from the streets of the ghetto, his strength bolstered by suffering. He is Napoleon, not Louis XVI. Dad is Beethovenian. When blinded in *Songs of Enchantment*, he is like Samson. He is also the vehicle for the human lesson contained in these books. Whether he is actively championing the Party of the Poor, or fighting a thug hired by its opponents in the open street, his views are far less significant than the intellectual and ethical courage he displays espousing them. Shortly after his father has chastised him, Azaro flees towards the spirit world in the company of a three-headed spirit. Hauled back to the world of the living, he lies recovering as his father kneels by the bed whispering the words: 'We are the miracles that God made to taste the bitter fruits of time. We are precious, and one day our suffering will turn into the wonders of the earth . . .' (FR 338).

In October 1991, when Okri was presented with his Booker Prize at a ceremony at the Guildhall in London, he stood in the glare of the television lights and read to an audience of millions his poem 'An African Elegy'. A versification of Dad's impassioned exhortation, it was to appear as the title piece to a volume the following year (AE 41). The effect struck home, since, though – in the poem if not in the novel – the sentiments proclaim their national origin, they also touch on a vein of stoicism necessary to every human life. If 'The Famished Road' sequence has a moral, Black Tyger's subdued homily – and the associated poem – are as close as we approach to it.

Black Tyger is a resonating chamber for literary echoes. His occupation gives a clue to the first of these, which again relates to Soyinka. As a porter and night-soil man, Dad corresponds to a well-known West African type: the carrier (FR 433). Derek

Wright reminds us that such human beasts of burden are common in African literature, where they sometimes perform the function of a scapegoat for the people's misfortunes.[10] The best-known anthropological treatment of this theme is to be found in J. G. Frazer's *The Golden Bough*;[11] its most prominent Nigerian literary representative is Eman, the much put-upon – but also heroic – scapegoat figure in Soyinka's early play *The Strong Breed*.[12] Again, one is struck by the divergences of treatment. Okri's is a lot bolder than Soyinka's: it also possesses a bravado occasionally verging on comedy. As a result, Tyger's occupation seems less an enactment of an obscure ethnological custom than the realization of a slice of human destiny.

The spelling of Tyger's name echoes a well-known poem by Blake:

> TYGER! Tyger! burning bright
> In the forests of the night,
> What immortal hand or eye
> Could frame thy fearful symmetry?[13]

Blake's song with its accompanying engraving – to which in *Songs of Enchantment* Dad's appearance is specifically compared (*SE* 123) – is an expression of awe at some elemental source of energy. It also, however, refers to a particular event: the September massacres of 1792 during the French Revolution when the revolutionary mob in Paris left a decisive mark on the mind of Europe. Okri's novel is set at a time of similar political disruption in the development of Africa. Black Tyger stands at its vortex. He is history in the making. All history, I think, not just Nigerian history.

The same dynamism and diversity apply to other characters. An easily illustrated example is the figure known as 'Green Leopard'. He first appears at the end of volume one as a brawny wrestler spawned by the desperation of the ghetto. In the teeth of general expectation, Black Tyger throws him. By the beginning of *Songs of Enchantment* Green Leopard has invaded Tyger's dreams: no longer in his human embodiment, but as a spectral great cat of the forest (*SE* 27). From there he re-enters the zone of Azaro's experienced reality, prowling through the township, slinking across Madame Koto's bar, insinuating himself into the doings of everyday. Which is he: wrestler, dream image, feline beast? At the times of his greatest potency, Green Leopard appears to be all three. One is tempted to talk less of a character than of an archetype of leopard-ness suffusing the text.

In no group of characters is this protean quality more evident than the womenfolk. Madame Koto is at once drab and exotic, accommodating and obstructive, aged and nubile. As the sequence progresses she turns into a personality of historic proportions, and a fertility goddess. At moments Azaro sees her as decrepit and time worn (FR 496; IR 199). Then, at a local knees-up, he finds himself dancing with an alluring and statuesque stranger in a red gown, her face 'crowded with laughter' (FR 172–3). He looks again. It is Madame Koto. If Dad is Samson Agonistes, Madame Koto is like a combination of Aretha Franklin and Winnie Mandela. Who holds the destiny of the neighbourhood and nation in her grasp? Madame Koto. Who brings electricity to this people in darkness? Madame Koto. Who acquires, and drives with superlative inaccuracy, the first car anybody has ever clapped eyes on? Madame Koto. In *Songs of Enchantment* Azaro has a vision of her as an elevated presence pressing on Black Tyger's head (SE 222–42). In *Infinite Riches* she boasts 'I sit on the head of my enemies' (IR 28). For what event are we waiting throughout the entire sequence? Madame Koto's rally for the Party of the Rich. When it arrives at the end of *Infinite Riches*, it is a riot of cosmic dimensions, a preternatural jamboree (IR 226–56). Then she dies, stabbed by her outraged proselytes (IR 271). Her coffin becomes a force of nature; no one can tie her down. Madame Koto is a perpetual reminder that anything can turn into anything at any time. She is also the living, breathing instance of that generative quality of *abiku*hood that is Okri's main contribution to the science of fiction. She is all women, and all people.

If Madame Koto takes her ideas from the surrounding culture whose chaotic energies she epitomizes, Mum improvises endlessly. Subservient and maternal in volume one, she soon turns into the mainstay of the family. At the beginning of *Songs of Enchantment*, Azaro suddenly announces, 'Mum is changing' (SE 43). A few pages later, we read, 'Dad wasn't quite sure how to deal with the new apparition that was Mum.' In her resentment at his mental disloyalty with Helen, she acquires a dark, brooding power. Yet, when Black Tyger is slammed in gaol for supposedly murdering Ade's father, it is his wife and her female friends who have him released (*IR* 20–3), confronting the very same policeman from whose house she rescued her son at the beginning of *The Famished Road*. Azaro's mother serves as a perpetual reminder of the muscle that West African women have often flexed at times of public crisis, then as now. The apex of her adaptability is the strike for Independence that she organizes soon afterwards, a movement that – at least for a while – softens and transforms the face of the struggle:

> Mum changed in our eyes. Her absence nourished her myth. Women of our street, noticing how their comrades were seizing the national stage in acts of boldness, became quarrelsome, and staged strikes against their husbands. They had meetings in which they discussed the formation of organizations, in which they discussed how they could help Mum's group. They made sure that I was fed, and bathed, and beautifully clothed. They fussed over me as if I had suddenly become a hero. They talked about politics all day long. The word politics took on a warmer meaning. (*IR* 34)

If Dad represents the visible and resistant might of this novel sequence, Mum is its invisible strength. He works with biceps flexed, she with secret grace.

A more elusive embodiment of female power is provided late in the sequence by the 'Rain Queen'. Okri first encountered this enigmatic but powerful personage in an anecdote recounted by Graham Greene to a meeting of the Oxford and Cambridge Club in 1989. Nine years later she appeared in *Infinite Riches*, where her story is told by Black Tyger to the recumbent and appreciative Azaro. The Rain Queen lives in an ancient tree in the southern hemisphere; she has sixteen wives and men and women pour to her shrine to pay homage. 'She can enter into the dreams of nations and of continents.' When she dies, she has a choice between eating of the fruit of a forbidden tree or climbing up into the realm of the gods. Nobody knows which route she took. 'Is Madame Koto a Rain Queen?' Azaro asks (*IR* 177). That night he dreams of them as one; behind, a red angel stands guard. When he asks Madame Koto, she takes her revenge by driving Mum insane, forcing her to endure a delirium that she herself has experienced at an earlier stage in the saga. Black Tyger is distraught; he takes his wife to the forest and deposits her near a 1,000-year-old *iroko* tree, evidently a surrogate for the Rain Queen's legendary habitation. She is rescued by the old woman of the forest, a recluse who works an intricate tapestry depicting the history of the continent and has absorbed some of the Queen's elemental powers.

We thus have not so much a set of female characters as a moving energy field attaching itself to a succession of women. The cult of enchantresses who snatch Azaro away to their island at the beginning of *The Famished Road* are the first to display it (*FR* 10–14), followed by Madame Koto, Azaro's mother, the 'spirit woman' with whom Azaro almost elopes (*FR* 307), the Rain Queen, and the solitary female weaver. An equivalent, stoical masculinity attaches itself to several of the male characters, who share this magnetism with Azaro's father. Wole Soyinka once famously remarked that 'a tiger does not bother to proclaim his tigritude, he pounces.'[14] Dad is the rippling embodiment of active 'tigritude' or tygritude. A parallel female essence – a *femitude* if you like – pervades the text in the vicinity of Madame Koto.

Along with this resourcefulness in Okri's portrayal of character goes a concomitant originality in his narrative methods. I will mention five. The first might be called a technique of delayed recognition. In a scene early in *The Famished Road*, Azaro visits a lorry park where labourers are carrying loads from the back of a mammy wagon. A man weighed down with far more than his body can bear implores his colleagues to load more on, then lurches and sways his way to disaster through the throng. A second porter takes the stand, accepting his burden with grace. He carries it with back straining, with a daring that approaches arrogance, but a *knowing* arrogance. It is Azaro's father (*FR* 148–9).

Azaro then wanders into the market. He notices a woman trader being bullied by thugs who force her to give up her stall. She yields, but in such a manner as to make her tormentors seen petty. Azaro looks again. It is his mother (*FR* 168–70). To what epiphanies of insight is Azaro privy at such moments? He learns that his parents are victims of economic forces that they will never control. He discovers that no crowd is faceless, that behind every statistic a story such as his own extends. He also acquires invaluable insight into his parents' being, the pressures that have made them what they are, the qualities they need to survive, the unglamorous yet mystical strength that supports them, and through which they support him.

An associated technique is one that we might term *reversed bathos*. Classic bathos, of course, occurs when heroism trips over itself into absurdity. In Okri the reverse often happens, as absurdity stumbles over itself to be converted, gloriously, into heroism. The reflex is beautifully etched in that scene in the lorry park, just before Azaro recognizes his father. At one point, the carrier who sways and zig-zags his way to collapse immediately before Black Tyger's more effectual effort almost turns into a buffoon (*FR* 145–6). Note the *almost*, for there lies the passage's clandestine message. The first carrier's defeat is extreme, but it is not ignominious, nor in Azaro's or the novelist's eyes does he feature as a failure. Okri has performed a highly individual artistic feat, parodying his serious meaning before calling attention to his deeper purposes. Another instance of such narrative redemption occurs towards the end of the book, during Dad's titanic contest with Green Leopard. Early in the contest, shortly after submitting his opponent to 'the mathematics of a higher beating' (*FR* 398), Tyger is reduced to practical risibility. He rises above it into sheer majesty. Thus the smile is wiped luxuriously off the face of the reader who arrives to mock and, like the crowd, stays to admire. The effect of these transitions is to interrogate the distinction between comedy and seriousness, the 'point' of all such episodes, the 'point' even behind 'points'. Much is conveyed by passages such as these, but nothing is contained by them. The sole guide to interpretation is continuation: read on.

The forward momentum of such episodes is much assisted by another narrative resource. We might call it Okri's technique of 'migrating consciousness'. Azaro, for example, is not just a soloist: he is also a chorus of selves, and a polyphonic chorus at that. To begin with he is very much a spirit child

(*FR* 7–9), seeing what others do not perceive: the ghosts emerging from the photographer's camera (*FR* 45–6), three men with six fingers to each hand (*FR* 77), an 'invisible' girl at Madame Koto's shebeen (*FR* 202). As time progresses, he develops an almost schizoid awareness, open to events on earth and beyond it at one and the same time. The resulting counterpoint reaches cacophonous levels during his temporary desertion with the three-headed spirit (*FR* 325–9), when he is able to observe his parents' reactions to his own absence. Such simultaneity of rendition is related to two other aspects of the narrative: the echoing of experiences between characters, and transferability of dreaming. In *Songs of Enchantment*, Mum and Madame Koto both disappear within a few pages of one another. At one point, as a peacock flaps around him, Azaro thinks that he has seen his mother in the bar; it is another woman who has somehow absorbed her persona: 'There's something like mum in there,' he informs his father (*SE* 37). Aspects of Dad's dream life infiltrate Azaro's, who in turn lends intimations to the nightly imaginings to his father. At its most intense, this somatic slippage feeds into a pool of nightly images, as if the entire nation were being stalked by Jungian archetypes. People, animals, and spirits invade another. Dad is a 'sulphurous tiger of light' (*SE* 20). When Azaro hits his head, it is Dad who cries out (*SE* 128). When struck on an earlier occasion, he hears the cry of a cat (*FR* 431). Dad reprimands Azaro for being blown off his stool by a woman's sneeze. It is a spirit that has sneezed (*FR* 298).

In the overall structure of the novel sequence, this sideways slippage is connected with a narrative configuration with which Okri had been experimenting at least since his story 'Converging City' from *Incidents at the Shrine*. Accordingly, it might be styled his technique of 'converging circles'. An early instance of it occurs in *Songs of Enchantment* when Azaro follows the blind old man into the forest 'circling round him as he passed the centres of secular power' (*SE* 146). An even more vivid instance is to be found in the chapters jointly entitled 'Circling Spirit' that introduce the second section of *Infinite Riches* (*IR* 83–95). Once again, the passage begins with a story told to Azaro: this time by Mum. It concerns a king so enraged by the croaking of frogs in his vicinity that he has them all slaughtered, instigating a plague of the mosquitoes on which the noisy amphibians had once fed. No sooner is the story told than the ghetto is infested by successive scourges of frogs, toads, snakes, spiders, wolves, and hyenas. Investigating their origin, Azaro is led into the depths of the forest, from which a forlorn cry resounds. It is caused, as the Chekovian echo reminds us, by the complaints of newly felled trees. He comes across the perpetrators: a team of timber contractors who brusquely order him away. Azaro flees to another part of the forest, where he comes across a young girl with one whole and one wooden leg, leaning against a trunk. She implores his assistance and climbs onto his back. They pass a female figure outside a hut: the hermit-like weaver at her craft.

The scene accelerates for several paragraphs. The girl, who can stand the crescendo of events no longer, calls for Azaro to stop. He cannot, his legs propelled forwards by some inexorable force. Only when the old woman stops weaving for a moment does everything jolt to a hault: Azaro, the girl, the fauna and flora around them. The girl disappears, and Azaro makes his way to where nine African labourers are working under the supervision of a couple of disenchanted expatriate foremen. The team has been hacking at the same stout iroko tree to no effect for two whole weeks. The white men sweat and curse in frustration as their underlings attribute the tree's obduracy to its indwelling spirit. Unable to stand the situation a moment longer, one of the expatriates yells 'Superstitious Africans!' The forest explodes in cacophonous echoes. Heard in a glade some distance away, they drive two woodcutters mad. They run bezerk as Azaro's ubiquitous consciousness pursues them.

At one level Azaro's 'spirit' is following every aspect of the action here – even those that he cannot physically see – through a process of rapt telepathy. At another, the 'circling spirit' is the focus of the narrative, which moves hither and thither, attracted by perceived affinities between events, accelerating, slowing down, pausing, and then setting out again in response to rhythms that successive episodes dictate. At yet another, the author is presenting us with a series of interlocked vortices, spirals of dramatic and mental movement that find their apotheosis in the 'circular' shape of the nation's history sewn into the old woman's tapestry. The motion conveyed is at one and the same time abstract and earthed in the experience of the people. It is an experiment that harks back, and back, and back.

To discern such scenes requires several readings. Your ears must bristle to pick out the distant echoes. The near-inaudibility, near-invisibility, is germane to an aesthetic best summed up by a sentence in Black Tyger's homily to his son: 'There is wonder here, and there is surprise in everything you cannot see.' The statement invokes the last of Okri's techniques that I would like to mention, though it is perhaps less a technique than a philosophy: *inverted mimesis*. In these books reality consists precisely in what cannot – at least under 'normal' circumstances at any rate – be perceived. Thus stated, the aesthetic – and the metaphysics and epistemology underlying it – are idealist or Platonic. Dad's statement, however, is also susceptible of a less dramatic interpretation. Though events and persons possess an undeniable materiality, there is an added element to sense data informing its actuality: roughly speaking, its significance or meaning. This insight is clearly applicable to Azaro, since, though his parents and neighbours can follow most of his movements, they are for the most part oblivious of his everlasting destiny and the throng of spirit companions that crowd around his head.

This almost mystical philosophy of signification means that we must treat with some caution the view of Okri's writing as divided into 'realistic' and 'esoteric' episodes, with phases of transition joining them. Such an approach, tempting at first reading, ultimately fails because it sets up the reader as the standard of authenticity. A more flexible and responsive account can be obtained if Azaro himself is adopted as the measure of possibility and verisimilitude. Only by taking Azaro's viewpoint with absolute seriousness can we, for example, make sense of the numinous presences that in other novels one would tend to write off as supernatural interlopers: the forest sprites, or the various-headed spirits who act as messengers to Azaro from the other world. In Okri, these visitants belong to the same order of being as other, apparently 'ordinary', characters. Indeed, some of the most memorable figures in the whole sequence – Helen, for example, with her following of beggars – are quite unclassifiable in terms of common-sense empiricism or, for that matter, run-of-the-mill theology.

At no juncture in the narrative is this inter-communion of essences bolder than in the climactic scene in *Infinite Riches* in which all of the barriers suddenly come crashing down. A procession of occult presences rides through the township like figures in an ancient freize or a painting by Hieronymous Bosch, like manifestations from Soyinka's independence play *A Dance of the Forests* or emanations from a visionary poem by Blake or Shelley (*IR* 240–77). Sinister perhaps, but oddly heartening as well.

The emotional effect of such transgression, such 'stepping across' ontological thresholds, is easy enough to appreciate. It is more difficult to understand the philosophy of verification that such an exercise involves. As it happens, in 1995, between the publication of the second and third novels of 'The Famished Road' sequence, Okri published a short but memorable book that clarifies this task.

7

The Invisible City, 1995–

> Blessed City, heavenly Salem,
>   Vision dear of peace and love,
> Who of living stones upbuilded,
>   Art the joy of heaven above,
> And with Angel cohorts circled,
>   As a bride on earth does move!
>
>> (Seventh-century Latin hymn,
>>   trans. John Mason Neale)
>
> Tolle lege, tolle lege
> [Take up and read, take up and read]
>
>> (St Augustine, *Confessions*, bk iii, ch. 12)

In Italo Calvino's novel *Invisible Cities*, published in 1972 but set 700 years earlier, the explorer Marco Polo, who after long journeying has arrived at the court of Mongolia, describes to the ageing Kublai Khan the various municipalities through which he has passed. The Emperor is weary, his kingdoms raddled, 'an endless, formless ruin'.[1] Polo's account consoles him, opening to his jaded consciousness cities of glass or flame, inverted cities, cities that lie in the depths of the sea. Lulled by the voice of his Venetian guest, the Khan abandons himself to these communities, each less probable than his own Xanadu: structures of stone or metal but also compounds of memory or desire, evoking pulses or moods. He does not guess, nor can Calvino's readers be sure, whether these environments exist on any map. The question is irrelevant, since each distils an aspiration of, or excavation into, the imagination and intellect. Polo's domes and steeples, his cupolas and loggias, are expressions of idealized longing or dread: utopias or dystopias embodied in evanescent shapes.

Calvino's novel is utterly postmodern and relativistic, but its project of envisaging the absolute city is as ancient as town-planning. St Augustine's 'civitas dei', his City of God, or Sir Thomas More's *Utopia*, have been only the most widely advertised, and vividly Christianized, of such metropolises of the mind. Actual cities, moreover, often serve – at least in the planning stage – as moral and political experiments as much as provisions for human settlement. Calvino's innovation inheres in his aestheticizing of a hypothetical impulse, a fictionalization of the suppositions implicit in such schemes as a sequence of shimmering forms.

It goes without saying that Calvino's enterprise, like all other mental reworkings of the urban space, is a response to – and critique of – the complex conurbations many of us live and work in. Okri has never been influenced artistically by Calvino, but the two authors undeniably share one important thematic starting point: the re-interpretation, perhaps the spiritualization, of the modern urban space. Okri's first two novels, his volumes of short stories, the first volume of 'The Famished Road' sequence, had portrayed Lagos and London in arresting colours. When in 1995 – between the second and third volumes of his trilogy – he produced a slender fable featuring a nameless protagonist and set in an imaginary island city, his readers might have been forgiven for thinking that he had momentarily turned aside from the pressures of interpreting the modern world. In fact, *Astonishing the Gods* is intimately related both to Okri's view of modernity, and to the works of his that we have examined so far.

Like most successful alternative communities, Okri's island is a place that nobody has visited, but that each of us recognizes in some portion of our mind. It is stranded miles from any conceivable continent, yet the details of its architecture, the sumptuousness of its fabric, mark it as faintly Italian. It could be Venice without its canals; though it could also be any Mediterranean or south European city state transformed by the unconscious into a zone of permanent potentiality. There are also aspects of it – like the lingering scent of 'ripening mangoes' in the streets (*AG* 7) – that seem tropical. Its most distinctive characteristic, however – the subtlety that distinguishes it from a dozen or so other imagined communities – consists in absences of a particular kind.

It is important to begin our discussion by employing a word like 'subtlety' rather than a more emphatic term such as 'significance', since Okri's purpose involves a rethinking of the whole process of interpretation. We have already seen how suspicious he has been of the diminishing force of names. In *Astonishing the Gods* this scepticism is extended to a much wider critique of hermeneutics: the process through which hidden though constant meanings may be ascertained from a situation or text. During the story the protagonist enjoys the services of three guides: a man, a child, and a woman. All of them stress the unavailability of any comprehensive clue to the island and its way of life. Soon after his disembarkation, the stranger is confused by the appearance of a hall of mirrors in front of the Great Basilica. When he comments on the resulting confusion of images, his first guide exhorts 'Retain your bewilderment. Your bewilderment will serve you well' (*AG* 11). Soon afterwards, the guide invites him to cross a bridge made out of mist that turns in quick succession into fire, water, air, and stone. Once across, the visitor remarks that the significance of the experience is lost on him. His guide replies, 'Understanding leads to ignorance, especially when it comes too soon' (*AG* 30). When the newcomer insists on his personal need to 'make sense' of what has happened, his companion further stresses the futility of any such attempt: 'When you make sense of something, it tends to disappear. It is only mystery which keeps things alive' (*AG* 30). Indeed, throughout the earlier part of the story the principal character's urge to know is treated as an aberrant – possibly a neurotic – impulse.

It would be easy to misconstrue this attitude, which at times seems to permeate the authorial voice, as the expression of anti-intellectual or anti-academic prejudice. In fact, the islanders hold thought and theory in very high esteem. In book three, for example, the visitor enters the municipal market. Its commerce is mental, and its merchandise consists of paradoxes (*AG* 74). Slightly earlier, he enjoys a vision of the whole metropolis as one great 'network of thought'. The national library stretches from shore to shore, and the colleges absorb much of the energy of the people, though few of the teachers or students do any talking:

The universities and the academies were also places where people sat and meditated and absorbed knowledge from silence. Research was a permanent activity, and all were researchers and appliers of the fruits of research. The purpose was to discover the hidden unifying laws of all things, to deepen the spirit, to make more profound the sensitivities of the individual to the universe, and to become more creative.   (*AG* 66)

At first sight, this determination by the citizens to discover some kind of universal open sesame appears to be in flagrant contradiction of the warning issued by the guide against his protégé's desire to understand. The distinction lies in the means and attitudes adopted. Paradoxical as it may seem – but does the town market not *deal* in paradoxes? – the truth each student is aiming for in these island faculties is one that will indeed explain everything, but only in a manner valid for him- or herself. The local theory of knowledge, in fact, corresponds less to what I have called hermeneutics – a term deriving from biblical exegesis and implying the existence of an orthodox, if veiled, truth – than to a heuristic science through which each individual interprets the world uniquely. Once found, this understanding will possess the familiarity of something already perceived but insufficiently appreciated. That, for example, is why the traveller is forced to pace the streets of the city several times. He has seen the sights already, but failed to internalize them: as his last guide will inform him, 'In this place, things lose their reality if you are not aware of them' (*AG* 104). This also is why the response of all three of his guides to his enquiries is to turn the questions back on him. This furthermore is why his very first guide asks him not to guess glibly at the significance of the bridge – do not, he is implying, snatch at meaning, or assume it to be uniform. We would do well to take his advice to heart whilst reading Okri's text.

Okri's prose in this book has been called 'oneiric' or dreamlike, and its vision surreal. In practice, the slightly disconcerting atmosphere of the story has less to do with such conventional qualities than with the attitude to meaning outlined above. Take, for example, the book's portrayal of topography and history. In night dreams incompatible environments often coincide; the setting of *Astonishing the Gods*, by contrast, is so topographically consistent that it could be drawn. At its centre lies a piazza with its chequered pattern of flagstones and its palace facing a house of justice across the square. On the left rises an equestrian statue with his rider and his sword; to its right a fountain gushing around an effigy of a sea-god. To the right of that again, in the very corner of the quadrangle, stands a statue of the great mother. A few yards from the palace gate there is a loggia or three-sided outhouse containing further statuary. Between stands the figure of the prophet-king. All of this sculpture and its associated architecture are in an elaborate Rococo style, which, however, has the opposite effect from usual. It creates lightness out of gravity, grace out of monumentality. History is real here – rather than that cliché, surreal – but it is not heavy. It is consistent but not insistent. It does not bear you down.

This soothing effect is at one with the attitude the visitor's successive guides aim to induce in him. The city is leisurely and confident; in a word – one of Okri's favourite epithets – it is 'serene'. Everything that happens to the traveller is designed to frustrate his eagerness to absorb the townscape in a hurry. To begin with, the visitor is anxious. He devours the place with the avidity of a tourist or a day tripper. Though he has dismissed the steamer that brought him, it is as if it is still impatiently waiting for him in the harbour. Gradually, in the care of his invisible ghosts, he learns to calm down, to take the city at its own pace, to probe its intricacies and contradictions. Stylistically this new mood, and the attentive feeling it induces in him, is conveyed by a dextrous use of synaesthesia, the device in which different senses are compared. When the stranger first enters the city it is night and the moonlight is 'flavoured' (AG 5). The first time he enters the piazza, 'he inhaled the fragrance of childhood, of sweet yellow melodies' (AG 7). Entering the city a second time, he becomes aware 'of a mood of orange jubilation' (AG 43). To begin with, these rapprochements between different sense worlds take him by surprise. By the end, they have become second nature. When, at the concluding tribunal, he is asked to reconsider the meaning of the bridge in the light of all that has happened, 'He wandered in the cool spaces of the question' (AG 155).

One of the six senses is highlighted in the discourse of the book. This, of course, is sight, which is privileged only so that it may be questioned. The visitor, himself invisible, comes from a land of invisibility. When he arrives, the inhabitants are invisible to him: in fact, despite notable exceptions – the fleeing woman in book three, for example, or the lecherous woman who almost seduces him in book four – this remains the case throughout. The book is thus concerned at a fundamental level with the ongoing debate in Okri's work about visibility and invisibility, a subject on which we touched in chapter four.

For various reasons visibility, and ways of shedding or re-establishing it, recur constantly in modern literature. The most celebrated expression of the theme is probably H. G. Wells's 'grotesque' romance, *The Invisible Man* (1901).[2] It concerns a chemistry student called Griffin who makes himself invisible out of scientific curiosity. The condition proves irreversible, and he spends the entire book trying to convince society at large – against which he develops a deep grudge – that, though they can no longer see him, he actually exists. Eventually, his foiled efforts lead to a life of criminality and to a tragic death, whereupon he becomes visible again. Half a century later the title and some of the preoccupations of Wells's work were echoed by the African American writer Ralph Ellison in his novel *Invisible Man*, published in 1952.[3] Ellison's novel follows the downward slide of its first-person narrator: an African American, he is expelled from a southern college, then migrates to Harlem, where, in the aftermath of a race riot, he literally goes to ground, withdrawing to a sewer illuminated by brilliant arc lights. Hiding from a society that refuses to acknowledge him, he subjects his body and mind to an unreal luminosity to convince himself – if not others – that he is in fact there. Both Wells and Ellison are interested in the effects of occlusion and exclusion – whether physical or social – in anonymous contemporary settings. Ellison gives this concern a racial slant, but it is clear from these very different novels that invisibility as such – whether physical or symbolic – is an idea of wide application. It might almost be said to be a condition of being modern.

At the end of the 1950s, visibility and invisibility were given a theoretical foundation by the French philosopher Maurice Merleau-Ponty (1908–61). A former colleague of Jean-Paul Sartre, with whom he famously quarrelled, Merleau-Ponty was worried that the distinction drawn in Western philosophy between the perceiver and the perceived had left individuals in a state of disembodied isolation. He adopted the suggestion proposed by his phenomenalist predecessor, the German philosopher Edmund Husserl, that human experience should be treated on its own terms and 'bracketed off' from the normal processes of doubt (does it exist? does it not exist?). But Merleau-Ponty also wished to go further by stressing the fleshly immediacy of all seeing. At the same time, he recognized that the data absorbed by our senses cannot possibly account for everything we register moment by moment. There are unseen ingredients in the way in which we construct the world.

On his death in May 1961, Merleau-Ponty left behind a rough draft of a book entitled *Le Visible et l'invisible* in which for several months he had been wrestling with these very problems. The clearest exposition of what he meant by the 'invisible' occurs in a working note written in November 1959:

> Meaning is *invisible*, but the invisible is not the contradictory of the visible: the visible itself has an invisible inner framework [*membrure*], and the invisible is the hidden counterpart of the visible, it appears only within it, it is the *Nichturpräsentierbar* [unpresented-aspect] which is presented to me as such within the world – one cannot see it and every effort to *see it there* makes it disappear, but it is *in the line of* the visible, it is its virtual focus, it is inscribed within it (in filigree).[4]

Merleau-Ponty's main example of this unpresented-aspect is the five-note phrase from the 'Vinteuil Sonata' heard by Swann during an evening concert in the first volume of Marcel Proust's *A la recherche du temps perdu*.[5] Swann is quite capable of analysing or even transcribing this recurring *motif*. The notes themselves, however, do not constitute the phrase, which possesses a form and meaning, 'a lining and a depth', that alone make it intelligible. This invisible – or rather inaudible – element, cannot be accounted for by the individual sounds to which Swann is listening, nor is it separable from them. It represents rather an internal unity without which they would constitute nothing but a sequence of – albeit pleasurable – noises. The form and meaning of the resulting phrase is integrated into Proust's novel, which repeatedly describes it.

Again, for Merleau-Ponty, Proust's meaning is far from exhausted by the words on the page, nor can it be severed from them. In the philosopher's homely image – applicable, I think, both to Vinteuil's score and to Proust's prose – 'the meaning is not on the phrase like the butter on the bread ... it is the totality of what is said'.[6]

It is not hard to infer the relevance of such a programme of ideas to the invisible cities described by Marco Polo in the novel by Calvino with which this chapter began. Calvino's cities, after all, must be literally visible, since Polo has observed them. But there is also something that he has witnessed without perceiving it with his bodily eyes: the inner coherence, justification, and personality of these towns, the filigree presence that makes each what it is. Construed in this light, Calvino's text is a meditation on the succession of all such hidden meanings, which, taken together, compose the reality of one visible city: Polo's home town of Venice.

Again, Okri's fiction has its own momentum and its own strong logic, and its semantics are caste in quite a different mould from those that I have been discussing. Yet no art exists in a vacuum, and the modernist debate about visibility and invisibility undeniably forms one strand in Okri's writing, albeit that he has extended in unique and unprecedented directions. In *Astonishing the Gods*, the physical fabric of the island city is itself quite visible. The stranger, after all, deepens his appreciation of it by perusing its squares and buildings ever more carefully. Its people, however, are invisible to him from start to finish. The reason is that in Okri's fable they represent the city's meaning that is secret and hidden, as true meaning always is from naked and prying eyes. If the stranger were able to see the inhabitants, he might very well misunderstand them, because he would mistake their mere physical appearance for the actuality of their presence. In Okri's imagined city, people attain visuality only when they become – or aspire to be – something other than themselves. A character who illustrates this law in the fable is the disconsolate and somewhat overdressed lady borne aloft on a litter in book three. The visitor enquires where she is going. She sadly replies, 'I am going where I can see people, and where people can see me' (*AG* 77). When he asks her what she means, she explains, 'I am going where there is some illusion.' Another victim to the cult of appearance is the lustful woman who wishes to make love to the visitor in book four. He stops himself just in time, probably because he realizes that, if he succumbs, he will not be loving *her* at all, but the phantom that is her body. By this stage in the story, the visitor has learned to distinguish between people's nature and their projected image. So complete is this revelation that we almost forget that he embarked on his travels out of distaste for his own invisibility and that of his people.

His new attitude entails a risk, of course. As the dwarflike figure that makes his appearance shortly after the visitor's rejection of the seductress warns him, 'This is a rigorous land. Everyone lives without illusions. It is exhausting' (*AG* 107). Despite these difficulties, the visitor is equipped for the challenge posed by the island city in a way in which other newcomers are not. There are various signs that this is the case, the most important being his awareness of the stately unicorn with an emerald horn striding through the streets shortly after his arrival (*AG* 11). As he is soon informed, the mere fact that he has observed this legendary beast is a sign of his innate sensitivity to the island and its lore.

What is it that qualifies this visitor where others have failed? It is because, born invisible, he is ultimately capable of absorbing a truth he has always known but suppressed. Though superficially disabling, to be unseen by others can, he realizes, serve as a condition of knowledge, even of beauty. The way of life on the island, which initially strikes the stranger as being a siesta of uncomplicated happiness, is predicated on suffering and its transcendence. Schooled in deprivation as he has been, this is a truth that – with a little external prompting – he appreciates without too much resistance. Unknown to himself, therefore, he harbours a moral privilege known only to the overlooked and the oppressed.

There is one more element to his instruction. Though his unseen guides communicate deeply with him, he soon realizes with astonishment that no language in the ordinary sense has passed between them. All along they have been relating 'beyond words' (*AG* 36). The islanders distrust language because they regard it as an extension of that name-calling to whose suspect tendencies I called attention in Chapter 1. *Astonishing the Gods* informs us of one additional aspect of the insufficiency of language. This has to do with personal identity: a reality that has a tendency to confound ordinary descriptive language. I, after all, am not what people say about me: I am not that shifting mass of colour, shape, sound, and gesture that is seen, and of which others speak. There is, moreover, one species of language that is relevant to the perceptions that others have of me, and quite another that is appropriate to the self that I know. Those whose appearance is taken for granted by themselves and by the world often fall into the error of taking their gossip-mediated identity or image as read. Those, on the other hand, whose presence is habitually ignored or slighted possess this intellectual advantage: they know the limits of seeing, and they respect the limits of language. It is this that connects invisibility in Wells's and Ellison's sense with the existential condition described by Merleau-Ponty or Calvino. Visually to be passed over is, potentially, to acquire a princely access to meaning.

The title, and some of the themes, of Okri's novel are echoed five years later in the closing moments of his hymn for the millennium, *Mental Fight*, where we read:

> In the kingdom of this world
> We can still astonish the gods in humanity
> And be the stuff of future legends.
>
> (*MF* 68)

The term 'anti-spell' in its title gives the clue to this poem, which is a way of outfacing Western – and more parochially – British – cynicism at a time of widespread cynicism and low collective 'self-esteem' ('I cannot', Okri once told me, 'join the carpers'). In its individual way it is a revolutionary work, as radical as the Romantic poets, who, towards the end of an exceptionally jaded eighteenth century, tried to inject a little self-love, wonder, and mystery into a literary world habituated to the world-weariness of Alexander Pope or, later, of Thomas Crabbe. Okri is aware of all these antecedents, but especially of Blake, from whose clarion call 'And did those feet in ancient time?', evoking an ideal Jerusalem, the general title of his poem is taken:

I will not cease from Mental Fight,
Nor shall my Sword sleep in my hand
Till we have built Jerusalem
In England's green & pleasant Land.[7]

Blake's potential and perfect city envisages a liberation of oppressed humanity such as Okri had embodied in his working-class hero Black Tyger, the indomitable pugilist of *The Famished Road*. In *Mental Fight* the limbering-up of one champion of the proletariat is transformed into a resurgence of all humankind from a collective slough of despond. The poem often seems strange, because, as readers of twentieth-century verse, we have grown so used to minimalism, obscurity, or narcissistic self-pity that we take these qualities as the hallmarks of poetry. Okri counters this drab contemporary mood by answering to several great poets of the past: to Blake, of course, but also to the Eliot of *The Four Quartets*, the sombre but elevating music of which pervades his performance. Okri's feat is to deploy this music, culled from a conservative – some would say a reactionary – poet, in an appeal instinct with spiritual insurrection.

Okri deeply admires Eliot, both as a fellow artist and as someone who, in his later years at any rate, pulled poetic articulation towards areas normally seen as the preserve of the visionary or mystic. Like *The Four Quartets*, *Mental Fight* is difficult to tie down because it belongs to a mode of expression that is halfway to being a mode of action. The Okri who wrote it is the man who in the mid-1990s devoted much of his time and energy to the cause of Ken Saro-Wiwa (1941–96), like himself a member of a minority group within Nigeria, executed in December 1996 after a mock trial under the venal government of General Abacha. In *A Way of Being Free* the essay 'Fables Are Made of This' is dedicated to Saro-Wiwa's memory (*WBF* 104–5). Like Christopher Okigbo – whose phrase it is – Saro-Wiwa is portrayed as being a 'town-crier', whom the world in general is glad to ignore. Also in *A Way of Being Free* Okri addresses Salman Rushdie, victim of a notorious *fatwa* by the then Iranian government, in a sequence of aphorisms entitled 'The Human Race if Not Yet Free' (*WBF* 49–61); it has something of the paradoxical, flash-in-the-pan quality to be found in works such as Blake's 'The Marriage of Heaven and Hell'. As in Blake, the sentiments have gravitas, but they also possess another property highly characteristic of their author: a measured, almost balletic, lightness of touch. They are vocalized towards Rushdie but they also resonate towards the iconoclastic daredevil that exists inside every artist who wishes from time to time to step from the plinth of mere public regard.

'In my beginning is my end' wrote Eliot in his second quartet, 'East Coker'.[8] Okri's essays and much of his poetry convey the futility of regarding the recognized artist and the youngster who first put pen to paper as separable beings. The faculty that unites them is the 'impish freedom' of which Okri speaks in the sixth aphorism of his open letter to Rushdie (*WBF* 51). Without it, the public man and the private dreamer are both doomed.

8

Beyond Words

Onto our forgotten selves, onto our broken images;
   beyond the barricades
Commandments and edicts, beyond the iron tables,
   beyond the elephant's
Legendary patience, beyond his inviolable bronze
   bust; beyond our crumbling towers

   (Christopher Okigbo, 'Elegy for Alto')

For here have we no continuing city . . .
   (Epistle to the Hebrews, 13: 14)

There is yet another permutation on invisibility with which *Astonishing the Gods* has to do, one that harks back to hints in Okri's earlier writing.[1] The recognition of talent sometimes involves a distortion of perception quite as extreme as those arising from obscurity. If you are unknown, or belong to a marginalized minority, your presence is largely ignored. Propelled into the limelight, you suddenly find your image and voice endlessly amplified through a cacophony of competing media. For the artist, the shift in perception can be alarming – all the more so since the inner self, the person who produced the works of the intelligence that provoked all this fuss in the first place, is simultaneously reduced to near-inaudibility. Signal its presence as this inner being might, the world is enamoured, not of *it*, but of a mask that, almost despite itself, the work has somehow spawned. As in the case of Courtney Pine, the young jazz saxophonist Okri heard performing in London in the mid-1980s, a new type of visibility and a strange form of invisibility dramatically coincide.[2]

Readers and camp followers often misunderstand this state of affairs, yet it is the artist who must live with the consequences. If your personal medium happens to be words, then the predicament is made more irksome by the fact that each and every statement made from now on, lured into a shiny megaphone of publicity, echoes through the public stratosphere in self-begetting sound bites. You are used to saying what you mean, and meaning what you say. Now everything that you say is at the mercy of a process of relentless simplification that a society of eager cultural consumers insists in treating as if it were you.

An anecdote may help illustrate this process, for it concerns an African writer whom Okri has long viewed as an exemplar both of a certain kind of embattled integrity and of the extreme difficulty of maintaining that stance in a world determined to misconstrue it. In October 1991 Okri came up to Cambridge as a Fellow Commoner in Creative Arts at Trinity College, where I was then teaching whilst writing a book on Proust.[3] One of his priorities soon became obvious: he wanted to ensure that the works of the Igbo writer Christopher Okigbo, supreme lyrical poet, classicist, and one of the great prophets of war in the twentieth century, should be better known in that distinguished – but in some ways rather insular – university. With this end in view we planned an evening of readings and talks entitled 'To Sow the Fireseed: A Celebration of Christopher Okigbo (1932–1967)'.[4] Ben was away for the couple of weeks preceding the event. In his absence the publicity was prepared by the erudite and attentive seventeenth-century scholar who ran the college's arts programme. Knowing Okri's distrust for cultural chauvinism of all kinds, he blazoned across each poster the famous disclaimer by Okigbo on refusing a prize for 'African Poetry' at the 1966 Festival of Black Arts in Senegal: 'There is no African Literature. There is good writing and bad writing that is all.' When Okri returned and saw the posters he was seriously disconcerted, not so much because he disagreed with the quotation, but because Okigbo's provocative and Shavian brickbat, aimed at a given bunch of bureaucrats at a particular moment in history, had been converted into a statement of absolute principle to which he was now expected to subscribe.

One logical response to such unavoidable distortion is to retreat beyond words to a space or discipline where meaning and thought still coincide. One such opportunity is offered by mathematics. Another is provided by that condition to which, according to Walter Pater, all art – and by extension all literature – aspires. I mean music, which was also one of Okigbo's great loves. Okri had always been attracted to both fields, without being professionally qualified in either. Trinity, where Isaac Newton was student and fellow, is famously mathematical; it also has a world-famous choir. Ben's stay there saw the composition of his essay 'Newton's Child'. It also gave him an opportunity to combine these two extra-literary interests of his. On the 350th anniversary of Newton's birth, he was invited by Michael Atiyah – Lebanese-born mathematician and President of the Royal Society – to write the words for an anthem to the seventeeth-century scientist. Set to music by the composer Richard Marlow, 'Newton Enigmas' was performed on Friday, 3 July 1992, at the opening of the Isaac Newton Institute for Mathematical Sciences, and published in *The Times* the following day.[5] The Newton it depicts is partly the experimenter of *The Optics*, and partly the 'ethereal self' hinted at by Wordsworth's description of his statue in the college ante-chapel, with its 'prism and silent face|The marble index of a mind for ever|Voyaging through strange seas of Thought, alone' to a place where even poetry and music cannot reach him:

> It is not the nature of Light
> That it grows
> But yours does
>
> Your life is your gospel
> You made time feed on earth
> As we all should
> But you did it long
> And kept your parables silent

One evening soon after his arrival I invited Ben to my room to listen to an audio cassette that I had just bought: an interpretation by Kyung Wha Chung and Radu Lupu of César Franck's Sonata in D for Violin and Piano. It is this piece of chamber music, transformed into the 'Vinteuil Sonata', that Proust describes obsessively in *A la recherche du temps perdu*. For the philosopher Merleau-Ponty, as we have already seen, it was a paradigm of invisible form. As the famous 'little phrase' – containing eight notes, though reduced by Proust to five – recurred in the violin part, a question hovered between us. Was it appropriate to translate this condition of absolute musicality into words of appreciation, a medium it had successfully transcended? Do you perform a service to the invisible by rendering it visible? The question answered itself.

But music does not have to have been made out of notes. Paradoxically perhaps, words too contain a non-verbal element, especially – though by no means exclusively – when employed in poetry. Oddly, though by no mean illogically, such higher harmonics are sometimes detected most acutely by readers or listeners who know the language concerned imperfectly. Earlier that year, Ben had fallen in love with another of Okigbo's governing passions: the poetry of Virgil. Not with that nationalistic saga *The Aeneid* so much as with the Roman agricultural round as depicted in the *Georgics*. When *Songs of Enchantment* was going through the press, he added a dedication to his father, followed by an epigraph from its second book 'felix, qui potuit rerum cognoscere causas' (happy is he who has been able to discern the causes of things).[6] It was the pastoral *Eclogues*, however, that I found Okri reading time after time when I called at his little office in Blue Boar Court. If anything in literature approaches the condition of music, it is surely these – on the face of it somewhat artificial – dialogues set in an imaginary and idyllic Arcadia. Okigbo once Englished the opening of the first eclogue – 'TITYRE, tu patulae recubans sub tegmine fagi' – as a canzone, to be accompanied by a flute.[7] Okri's inspiration was a diapason passage in the fourth:

> Ultima Cumaei venit iam carminis aetas;
> magnus ab integro saeclorum nascitur ordo.
> iam redit et Virgo, redeunt Saturnia regna;
> iam nova progenies caelo demittitur alto.
>
> Now is fulfilled the Sybil's ancient strain;
> The world's great age enjoys a second birth.
> A maid returns; Saturn resumes his reign;
> A celestial generation walks once more on earth.[8]

Virgil's lines were written in 40BC to celebrate the dynastic marriage between Mark Anthony and Octavia, daughter of the poet's patron, the future Emperor Augustus. In the Middle Ages they were frequently seen as prophetic of Christ's birth. In 1821, during the Greek War of Independence, Shelley translated the second line in the climactic chorus of his liberation drama, *Hellas*: 'The world's great age begins anew.'[9] For Okri, I think, they evoked – and still evoke – a perpetually deferred hope lying beyond the entrenched divisions of the present.

In October 1996 Okri was invited by the BBC to make a programme for their series *Great Railway Journeys*.[10] He chose to go to Greece: to the Arcady of the *Eclogues*. On the way he travelled to the heel of Italy, where he stood before the monument to Virgil in Brindisi and indicated for his television audience its inscription from the tenth Eclogue, tarnished somewhat by time. 'Omnia vincit amor' (Love conquers all).[11]

There was a further element to the attraction. Virgil's poetry represents a potent instance of what, in his piece on Newton, Okri calls 'the law of subliminal effect'. Sometimes in the *Eclogues* the sound appears to operate almost independently of the meaning; at other times the match between sense and euphony is so smooth that its music seems to be what the poetry is expressing. For the reader such effects are unconscious, though for the author they are the result of careful technique. In Latin they frequently have to do with interplay between vowels. In all languages they involve a meticulous choice of diction and word order. In 'Newton's Child' Okri confides:

> It is amazing how much writing is a combination of mathematics and musical composition, of reason and aesthetics. It is also amazing how much of writing is rewriting; how much is instinctive; how much is simple logic, and the operation of so many secret and invisible laws. Take, for example, the law of visuality – the words you actually see on the page. There is, to give another example, the law of subliminal effect – words that you don't notice but which make you see things more acutely. (*WBF* 24)

Okri had just devoted a year to recasting his early novel *The Landscapes Within* as *Dangerous Love*. He spoke with an awareness of craftmanship tingling in his fingers. The alterations – some of them very minor – that he had introduced into this apprentice work all exemplify one or both of the two laws spelled out in the above paragraph, where they are presented as complementary rather than opposites.

The law of visuality, for example, corresponds to a condition in which the verbal medium is almost translucent. You come across this quality in much traditional African orature and in the novels of Achebe, and you find it in a few notable European authors of the remote or nearer past. Some poets excel at it (Okigbo, for instance, reading whom is like staring into a clear pool, which dizzies the head *because* it is so clear), as do some playwrights. I once spent the whole of a protracted train journey between Calais and Paris arguing with Ben about the respective merits of Ibsen (his choice) and Chekhov (mine). The dispute revolved around this question: which of these two supreme dramaturges is least ostentatious in his art? My line of defence was that Chekhov's subtlety is apparent in every well-crafted scene. Okri countered that the Russian's weakness inhered in this very fact. How can a writer conceivably be unostentatious when you notice his reticence? 'Have you ever,' he asked me rhetorically as our carriage swayed across Picardy, '*noticed* how unobtrusive Ibsen's plays are?' 'No,' I answered truthfully. 'Well then . . .'

Amongst novelists the master in this respect is Okri's admired Tolstoy. When you are reading *Anna Karenin*, do you care a dried fig for Tolstoy's narrative voice? Of course, you may admire it in restrospect. Such plain, objective-seeming writing is nowadays sometimes unfairly called 'impersonal narration' (how could it ever possibly be that?), or, even more confusingly, the 'declarative style' (what exactly is it supposed to be declaring?). In fact, it is achieved transparency.

Which, at least in Okri's view, is very different from simplicity, or even quietness. I once outraged him across the telephone by defending some contemporary British novelists of the Anita Brookner tendency. There was a sapient snarl on the other end of the line. 'Yes,' Okri replied in equitable tones. 'Writing like that always goes down very well. You know what it is saying?' His voice dropped to a booming whisper: '*Look* how *understated* I am!'

Beauty of execution cannot therefore be reduced to any such rule of thumb as 'showy writing is bad' or 'self-effacing writing is good'. Pleasure and instruction may be found in both. In every case, however, it will be the result of a shifting negotiation between form and content, sense and meaning, the artistically visible and the artistically invisible. The passage from 'Newton's Child' goes on:

> Some writing is forceful, ambitious and immediate: it is all there, it is sensual. Another kind of writing appears simple, does not seem to add up to much on the page, and performs no somer-saults. We think of one kind of writing as better, and sometimes we are wrong, and sometimes we are right. When they work, both kinds of writing are gifts, and both are magical. (*WBF* 24)

Words do not therefore enchant us by beating their chests. But they are not necessarily any more convincing when they hum gently in a corner. By shrinking in volume they may very well be implying, with unseemly forthrightness, '*Look* how *demure* we are.' This is exhibitionism by default, inverted stridency. The aesthetic of invisibility is quite distinct from this, as are the politics of invisibility.

Visible art, visible politics, are symptoms of an anxious, self-regarding energy. Reverting to an earlier theme, they are ways of naming, claiming, and declaiming. Again to adapt Achebe's proverb from *Things Fall Apart*, writing of this kind is the stylistic equivalent not of flying, or even of perching, but of flapping your wings about, or in some instances of preening or ruffling them self-consciously. The aeronautic prospects are not favourable. In politics the final result is more dramatic. To quote Okigbo once more, the likely result is 'an iron dance of mortars'.

What is the alternative? It is a particular way of attending to stories, of telling them so profoundly or listening to them so attentively that, to quote Okri's paraphrase of T. S. Eliot, 'you become the story while the story lasts' (*WBF* 48). Thus understood, narrative is a mode of reconciliation, of healing, and of self-forgetfulness. Narrative, in a nutshell, is the opposite of naming. As you tell or listen, your nationality or affiliation falls away. Of course, at one level your ethnic or cultural background must influence your response to the linguistic medium. This is one reason why transparency in the telling can be not simply an artistic, but a moral and political

101

obligation as well. Once beyond words, tellers and listeners are neither Hausas nor Igbos, Romans nor Greeks. For good or for evil, they become the tale. This partly explains why, as Okri constantly points out, similar stories are forever reappearing in very different contexts, and amongst superficially unrelated peoples (*WBF* 45). Stories are nation-blind. Attend a performance of *Hamlet* or *The Winter's Tale* in, say, Senegambia, and you will observe this fact at close quarters. Only authors who have looked into the metallic face of war sufficiently crave such metamorphic power. 'Shakespeare', Okri once asserted, 'is an African writer'.[12]

And, once beyond the conflict and the divisions, where do the stories lead? Okri has sometimes been very close to what theologians call 'the four last things'. Death, a transitional point, is one of them. Some of these experiences I will not talk about. However, in Cambridge, Okri's office was next to that of the distinguished scholar of comparative religion, Canon John Bowker, author of *The Meanings of Death*. One evening he discovered this expert on the religious significance of mortality dying in his darkened room. Okri raised the alarm. The following year the Canon reissued his book. 'Truth', it said, 'can therefore be told in fiction as well as in fact, by way of poetry as well as by way of proof.'[13]

And the object of truth? Black Tyger puts it well in *Songs of Enchantment*: 'Stories can conquer fear' (*SE* 46). Moreover, I do not believe that I ventriloquize for my subject too drastically if I respond with a vision glimpsed by Okigbo in the last of his 'poems prophesying war': 'Elegy for Alto'. It was composed a few months before the outbreak of the Nigerian Civil War, and his own violent death. Listen then to Okigbo's alto sax. 'Beyond the barricades|Commandments and edicts', it sings, a fresh rhythm pulses:

> AN OLD STAR departs, leaves us here on the shore
> Gazing heavenward for a new star approaching;
> The new star appears, foreshadows its going
> Before a going and a coming that goes on forever . . .

Notes

CHAPTER 1. A DANCE OF DESCRIPTIONS

1. The original sermon was delivered at Sunday evensong on 30 May 1993 at the invitation of the Dean of Chapel and New Testament scholar, the Revd Dr Arnold Browne.
2. For the philosophical bias in Okri's work, see also 'The Joys of Storytelling III', proposition 41, in *WBF* 117: 'The African mind is essentially abstract, and their storytelling is essentially philosophical.'
3. Chinua Achebe, *Things Fall Apart* (London: Heinemann Educational Books, 1958), 18. Cited by Okri in *WBF* 103, where the reference is to free creatures living beyond the reach of tyranny. By implication, Okri's own fleet-winged approach to art offers a similar resistance.
4. Ludwig Wittgenstein, *Tractatus Logico-Philosophicus*, ed. with trans. D. F. Pears and B. F. McGuiness (London: Routledge & Kegan Paul, 1961). Proposition 3.144, p. 23.
5. *Mungo Park's Travels in Africa*, ed. with Introduction by Ronald Miller (London: Dent, 1954), 305.
6. See Obaro Ikime, *Niger Delta Rivalry: Itsekiri–Urhobo Relations and the European Presence 1884–1936* (London: Longman, 1969).
7. For the delicate balance of power in Warri during this period, see Obaro Ikime, *Merchant Prince of the Niger Delta: The Rise and Fall of Nana Olomu, Last Governor of the Benin River* (London and Ibadan: Heinemann, 1968), and Obaro Ikime, *The Member for Warri Province: The Life and Times of Chief Mukoro Moroe of Warri, 1890–1948* (Ibadan: Institute of African Studies, 1977).
8. The British, for example, continued to misrepresent Nigerian politics in this way. As late as 1999 the former Labour Party Deputy Leader Roy Hattersley interviewed Okri for the *Guardian* newspaper. In the resulting article this resolutely

patriotic Yorkshireman referred to the Urhobo people as the 'Yoruba', thus confounding one of Nigeria's smaller and least influential ethnic groups with one of its largest and most powerful ('Ben Okri: A Man in Two Minds', The Guardian Profile, *Guardian*, 21 Aug. 1999, p. 6). One can just imagine the fuss had the *Guardian* referred to Baron Hattersley of Sparkbrook as a 'Lancastrian'.

9. For the significance of 'fugue' in Okri's thinking, where it means both 'flight' and a musical-cum-literary structure, see *WBF* 46.

10. Bill Ashcroft, Gareth Griffiths, and Helen Tiffin, *The Empire Writes Back: Theory and Practice in Post-Colonial Literatures* (London and New York: Routledge, 1989).

11. Sir David Brewster, *Memoirs of the Life, Writings, and Discoveries of Sir Isaac Newton* (Edinburgh: Constable, 1855), ii, 407. Brewster is illustrating Newton's 'great modesty'.

CHAPTER 2. AMONG THE SPIRIT CHILDREN, 1959–1978

1. Chinua Achebe, *Things Fall Apart* (London: Heinemann, 1958).

2. Quoted in Roy Hattersley, 'Ben Okri: A Man in Two Minds', The Guardian Profile, *Guardian*, 21 Aug. 1999, 6.

3. *Africa: A Who's Who*, 1141.

4. Bar Association Records, London.

5. Hattersley, 'Ben Okri: A Man in Two Minds', 6.

6. Gani Fawehinmi, *Bench and Bar in Nigeria* (Lagos: Law Publications Ltd, 1988), 785, 871.

7. For which see Wole Soyinka, *The Man Died* (London: Rex Collings, 1972).

8. Quoted in Nicholas Shakespeare, 'Fantasies Born in the Ghetto', *The Times*, 24 July 1986, 13.

9. Quoted in ibid.

10. For an admittedly partisan account of the British role in this debacle, see Auberon Waugh and Suzanne Cronje, *Biafra: Britain's Shame* (London: Michael Joseph, 1969). Waugh named one of his children 'Biafra'.

11. For the educational development of the Urhobo during the immediate post-war period, see Obaro Ikime, *The Member for Warri Province: The Life and Times of Chief Mukoro Moroe of Warri, 1890–1948* (Ibadan: Institute of African Studies, 1977).

12. In relation to which, note Okri's comment to the New York journalist Alan Ryan in July 1992: 'Dickens' characters are Nigerians' ('Talking with Ben Okri', *Newsday*, 19 July 1992).

13. Quoted in ibid.
14. Shakespeare, 'Fantasies Born in the Ghetto', 23.

CHAPTER 3. RESPONSIBILITIES: FICTIONS, 1978–1982

1. Exod. 20: 4.
2. Chinua Achebe, *Things Fall Apart* (London: Heinemann, 1958), 3–6. The parallel with Jonan's father is uncanny: 'When Unoka died,' we read on page 6, 'he had taken no title at all, and he was heavily in debt'.
3. In the following discussion the wording of the quotations is, by and large, taken from *The Landscapes Within*. I discuss the effect of the stylistic changes in *Dangerous Love* in Chapter 8 below.
4. Plato, *The Republic*, bk III, 398. One should add, in fairness to Plato, that Socrates insists on the dissident poet being treated with the utmost courtesy, anointed with myrrh, and crowned with fillets of wool – before being asked to leave.
5. *Yeats's Poems*, ed. A. N. Jeffares with an appendix by Warwick Gould (London: Macmillan, 1989), 196. Yeats attributes the saying 'to an old play', which, however, has never been discovered.
6. Wole Soyinka, *The Interpreters* (London: Heinemann, 1965).

CHAPTER 4. THE VISIBLE CITY, 1978–1991

1. Alan Ryan, 'Talking with Ben Okri', *Newsday*, 19 July 1992.
2. Nicholas Shakespeare, 'Fantasies Born in the Ghetto', *The Times*, 24 July 1986.
3. Ben Okri, 'No Room in the Inn', *New Statesman*, 20–27 Dec. 1985, 33.
4. Iris Murdoch, *Under The Net* (1954; London: Penguin, 1960), 24.
5. Okri, 'No Room in the Inn', 33.
6. James Joyce, *Dubliners* (1914; London: Grafton, 1977), 201.
7. Robert Fraser, 'The Dream Book', i. 'December 1983–May 1985', 23; entry for 14 Jan. 1984.
8. Robert Fraser, 'The Dream Book', iii. 'December 1986–May 1987', 29; entry for 5 Jan. 1987.
9. Ben Okri, 'Gifted . . . and Black', *New Statesman*, 17 Oct. 1986, 36.
10. I discuss Ellison's novel – and the related issue of 'invisibility' – in Chapter 7 below.
11. Ben Okri, 'Meditations on Othello', review of Royal Shakespeare Company production, *West Africa*, 1, 23 Mar. 1987, 562–4; 2, 30 Mar. 1987, 9. Collected in *WBF* 71–87 as 'Leaping out of Shakespeare's Terror'.

12. Ben Okri, 'Labelled', *New Statesman*, 15 Mar. 1985, 30.
13. For an informed résumé of Marechera's life and work, see Flora Veit-Wild (ed.), *Dambudzo Marechera: A Source Book on his Life and Work* (London: Hans Zell, 1992).
14. For the question of Marechera's reputation – and some rewarding insights into his work – see Flora Veit-Wild and Anthony Chennells (eds), *Emerging Perspectives on Dambudzo Marechera* (Trenton, NJ: Africa World Press, 1998).
15. Robert Fraser, 'The Dream Book', iii. 'December 1986–May 1987', 48–9; entry for 27 Jan. 1987.
16. The exact date was 14 August 1987. My obituary for Marechera appeared in the *Independent* newspaper on 25 August, p. 9. For an account of 'Marechera's Last Months', as viewed from a Zimbabwean perspective, see Veit-Wild (ed.), *Dambudzo Marechera*, 375–8; for the posthumous cult that has gathered around his name, see ibid. 379–92. Several of Dambudzo's typescripts have been published in the intervening years, notably *The Black Insider* (London: Lawrence & Wishart, 1992).

CHAPTER 5. MICROCOSMS: FICTIONS, 1982–1998

1. In 'Fantasies Born in the Ghetto' (*The Times*, 24 July 1986), Okri talks of the demands placed on the short story by the reader: 'You can't read Joyce's *Dubliners* casually: you'd be bored stiff.'
2. This sort of delayed recognition or epiphany is a technique that Okri came to use with increasing effect. For later examples, see p. 77.
3. *PEN New Fiction 1*, ed. Peter Ackroyd (London, Melbourne, and New York: Quartet Books, 1984), 83–95. Six years later the story was reprinted by the late Auberon Waugh in his *Literary Review*, 34 (1990), 78–87.
4. Peter Ackroyd, *Dickens* (London: Sinclair-Stevenson, 1990).
5. Peter Ackroyd, *London: A Biography* (London: Chatto & Windus, 2000).
6. Again, for later uses of this technique, see pp. 53 and 79.
7. 'History is a nightmare from which I am trying to awake' is Stephen Daedalus' sentiment in the 'Nestor' chapter of Joyce's *Ulysses*.
8. A fragment of it appeared under that title in *West Africa*, 20 Feb. 1984, 1–8.
9. *New Statesman*, 15 Feb. 1985, 26–8. After its appearance in *Incidents at the Shrine*, it was reprinted in *West Africa*, 25 Aug. 1996, 1783–6.

10. See Robert Fraser, *Lifting the Sentence: A Poetics of Postcolonial Fiction* (Manchester and New York: Manchester University Press, 2000), 83–4.

11. The term 'liminal' in that sense was coined by the American anthropologist Victor Turner in such works as *The Forest of Symbols* (Ithaca, NY: Cornell University Press, 1967) and the essay 'Variations on the Theme of Liminality', in Sally F. Moore and Barbara Myerhoff (eds), *Secular Ritual* (Amsterdam: Van Gorcum, 1977). For liminality in Okri, see also Ato Quayson, *Strategic Transformations in Nigerian Writing: Rev. Samuel Johnson, Amos Tutuola, Wole Soyinka, Ben Okri* (Oxford: James Currey, 1997), 57–8, 87–8.

12. Tutuola's English language tale was published by Faber & Faber in 1952 at the instigation of T. S. Eliot. It draws extensively on Yoruba folklore as transmitted through the novels of an earlier vernacular Yoruba author, Chief D. O. Fagunwa. For the influence of Tutuola on Okri, see Quayson, *Strategic Transformations in Nigerian Writing*, 17, 102–3, 116–18, 120, 130–1, 136–7, 143.

13. Quayson, *Strategic Transformations in Nigerian Writing*, 116.

14. For a detailed discussion of the Orpheus and Eurydice myth in African literature, see Jane Wilkinson, *Orpheus in Africa* (Rome: Editions Bulzoni Editore, 1990).

15. Christopher Okigbo, *Labyrinths with Path of Thunder* (London: Heinemann, 1971), repr. in Christopher Okigbo, *Collected Poems* (London: Heinemann, 1986).

16. Robert Fraser, *West African Poetry: A Critical History* (Cambridge and Boston: Cambridge University Press, 1986), 127.

17. First published in *West Africa*, 7 Feb. 1983, 1783–6.

CHAPTER 6. 'WHEN THE ROAD WAITS, FAMISHED', 1991–1998

1. For the early critical reception of *The Famished Road*, see Harvey Porlock, 'On the Critical List', *Sunday Times*, 14 July 1991, section 6 (Books), 6.

2. The most incisive attempt to attach the first two books of the sequence to a 'folkloric paradigm' occurs in Ato Quayson, *Strategic Transformations in Nigerian Writing: Rev. Samuel Johnson, Amos Tutuola, Wole Soyinka, Ben Okri* (Oxford: James Currey, 1997), 121–52. An intelligent reading of the same volumes (and of *AG*) as pertaining to a localized variety of magic realism (which she in turn views as a subcategory of postmodernism) can be

found in Jo Dandy, 'Magic and Realism in Ben Okri's *The Famished Road*, *Songs of Enchantment* and *Astonishing the Gods*: An Examination of Conflicting Cultural Influences and Narrative Traditions', in *Kiss and Quarrel: Yoruba/English, Stategies of Mediation* (Birmingham University African Studies Series No. 5; Birmingham: Centre of West African Studies, 2000), 45–63.

3. Wole Soyinka, *Idanre and Other Poems* (London: Methuen, 1967), 10–11.

4. First produced by the Stage Sixty Company at Joan Littlewood's Theatre Royal, Stratford East, in September 1965. Wole Soyinka, *Collected Plays* (Oxford: Oxford University Press, 1973).

5. John, 11: 43.

6. John Pepper Clark, *A Reed in the Tide* (London: Longman, 1965), 5.

7. Soyinka, *Idanre*, 28.

8. Salman Rushdie, *Midnight's Children* (London: Jonathan Cape, 1981).

9. The grammatical technique and the preoccupation with the 'Way' are reminiscent of the novel *Two Thousand Seasons* (London: Heinemann, 1979) by the Ghanaian writer Ayi Kwei Armah.

10. Derek Wright, *Ayi Kwei Armah's Africa: The Sources of his Fiction* (London: Hans Zell, 1989), 77–8, 135–6, 147.

11. Sir James Frazer, *The Golden Bough: A Study in Magic and Religion*, part VI, 'The Scapegoat' (London: Macmillan, 1913), *passim*.

12. Soyinka, *Collected Plays*, i.

13. *The Poetry and Prose of William Blake*, ed. Geoffrey Keynes (London: Nonesuch, 1927), 73.

14. The remark is more often quoted that sourced. The occasion was the African Writers' Conference at Makerere University, Kampala, Uganda, in 1962. See Jahneinz Jahn, *Neo-African Literature*, trans. Oliver Coburn and Ursula Lehrburger (New York: Grove, 1968), 266.

CHAPTER 7. THE INVISIBLE CITY, 1995–

1. Italo Calvino, *Invisible Cities*, trans. William Weaver (London: Vintage, 1972), 5. Originally published as *Le città invisibili* (Turin: Giulio Einaudi editore, 1972).

2. H. G. Wells, *The Invisible Man: A Grotesque Romance* (London: George Newnes, 1901).

3. Ralph Ellison, *Invisible Man* (London: Victor Gollancz, 1953). First published in New York in 1952.

4. Maurice Merleau-Ponty, *Le Visible et l'invisible* (Paris: Gallimard, 1961), 269. The translation quoted is from *The Visible and the*

Invisible, trans. Alphonse Lingis (Evanston, Ill.: Northwestern University Press, 1968), 215.

5. Marcel Proust, *A la recherche du temps perdu* (Paris: Gallimard, 1987), i. 209–11.

6. Merleau-Ponty, *Invisible et l'invisible*, 198; *The Visible and the Invisible*, 155.

7. *The Poetry and Prose of William Blake*, ed. Geoffrey Keynes (London: Nonesuch, 1927), 464–5.

8. T. S. Eliot, 'East Coker', *The Complete Poems and Plays* (London: Faber, 1969), 177, l. 1.

CHAPTER 8. BEYOND WORDS

1. See Chapter 4, pp. 40–41.

2. For an account of some of these embarrassments, see Jonathon Green, 'Ben Okri Reflects on a Year as the Miss World of Bookdom', *The Times*, 13 Oct. 1992, final edn, 14.

3. Robert Fraser, *Proust and the Victorians: The Lamp of Memory* (London: Macmillan, 1994).

4. The Old Combination Room, Trinity College, Cambridge, Monday, 4 May 1992.

5. Ben Okri, 'Newton Enigmas', *The Times* (Saturday Review), 4 July 1992, 41. Compare and contrast Wordsworth, *The Prelude* (1850), iii, ll. 61–3. The Isaac Newton Institute opened its doors in October of that year with a three-year research programme into Low Dimensional Typology, Quantum Field Theory, and Dynamo Theory. It was at the Institute on Wednesday, 23 June of the following year that Andrew Wiles announced his solution to Fermat's last theorem. See p. x. For Okri on Chaos Theory, see *WBF* 102.

6. *Georgics*, ii. 490. *SE*, p. v.

7. First published as 'Song of the Forest', *Black Orpheus*, 11 (1962), 5. Translating *Eclogues*, i. 1–5. Printed as the first of 'Four Canzones, 1957–1961', in Christopher Okigbo, *Collected Poems*, ed. Adewale Maja-Pearce (London: Heinemann, 1986), 8.

8. *Eclogues*, iv. 4–7. Excuse my verse translation.

9. Percy Bysshe Shelley, *Poetical Works*, ed. Thomas Hutchison (Oxford: Oxford University Press, 1970), 477.

10. 'London to Arcadia', *Great Railway Journeys*, producer Jonathon Stedall, BBC2, Wednesday, 9 Oct. 1996, 9.30 p.m.

11. *Eclogues*, x. 69. I find it amusing that my mother-in-law, bred in the puritanical Welsh valleys, chose to remember this sentence as 'Omnia vincit labor' (Work conquers everything).

12. Quoted in Alan Ryan, 'Talking with Ben Okri', *Newsday*, 19 July 1992, with particular relation to Falstaff.
13. John Bowker, *The Meanings of Death* (Cambridge: Cambridge University Press, 1993), 210.

Select Bibliography

WORKS BY BEN OKRI

Novels

Flowers and Shadows (Drumbeat, No. 20; Harlow: Longman, 1980; reissued as a Longman African Classic, 1989).

The Landscapes Within (Drumbeat, No. 38; Harlow: Longman, 1981; reissued as a Longman African Classic, 1982).

The Famished Road (London: Jonathan Cape, 1991; London: Vintage, 1992; New York: Anchor Books, 1993; New York: Doubleday, 1996).

Songs of Enchantment (London: Jonathan Cape, 1993).

Astonishing the Gods (London: Phoenix House, 1995; Boston: Little, Brown, 1995).

Dangerous Love (London: Phoenix House, 1996).

Infinite Riches (London: Phoenix House, 1998).

In Arcadia (London: Weidenfeld and Nicholson, 2002).

Starbook (London: Rider Books, 2007)

Collections of Stories

Incidents at the Shrine (London: Heinemann, 1986; Boston: Faber, 1987; London: Vintage, 1993).

Stars of the Late Curfew (London: Secker & Warburg, 1988; London: Penguin, 1988; New York: Viking, 1989).

Volumes of Essays

Birds of Heaven (London: Phoenix House, 1996).

A Way of Being Free (London: Phoenix House, 1997).

Collections of Poetry

An African Elegy (London: Jonathan Cape, 1992; London: Vintage, 1997).

Mental Fight (London: Phoenix House, 1999).

Uncollected Stories

'In Another Country', *West Africa*, 25 Apr. 1981, 873–5.

'Fires Next Time Are Always Small Enough', *West Africa*, 25 Apr. 1983, 1020–1.

'A Prayer for the Living', *New York Times*, 29 Jan. 1993 (final edn); *Toronto Star*, 27 Feb. 1994 (metropolitan edn).

Uncollected Essays

'The Problems of Young Writers', *Daily Times* (Lagos), 10 Aug. 1978, 20.

Review of Amos Tutuola, *The Witch Herbalist of the Remote Town*, in *West Africa*, 14 Feb. 1983, 429–30.

'Out of Silence' (review of Peter Fryer, *Staying Power*), in *New Statesman*, 25 May 1984, 26.

'Colouring Book' (review of Alice Walker, *In Search of Our Mother's Gardens*), in *New Statesman*, 22 June 1984, 24.

Review of V. S. Naipaul *et al.*, *Finding the Centre*, in *Africa*, 154 (1984), 49.

Review of Ada Ugah *et al.*, *Song of Talakawa*, in *Africa*, 155 (1984), 53.

'Labelled', *New Statesman*, 15 Mar. 1985, 29–30.

'Survivor's Testament' (review of Ellen Kuzwayo, *Call Me Woman*), in *West Africa*, 7 June 1985, 31–2.

'No Room in the Inn', *New Statesman*, 20–27 Dec. 1985, 33.

'Lagos Lament', *New Statesman*, 9 May 1986, 35.

'Gifted . . . and Black', *New Statesman*, 17 Oct. 1986, 36.

'Soyinka: A Personal View', *West Africa*, 27 Oct. 1986, 2249–50.

'On Art and the Human Spirit' (review of Wole Soyinka, *Art, Dialogue, Outrage*), in *Third World Quarterly*, 11/1 (Jan. 1989), 175–7.

'A Saturday Service', *West Africa*, 11 Apr. 1988, 642–3.

Achebe, Chinua, Michelson, G. F., Okri, Ben, Pinter, Harold, Rush, Norman, Sontag, Susan, and Stone, Robert, 'The Case of Ken Saro-Wiwa' (Letter), *New York Review of Books*, 20 Apr. 1995, 71.

'Three Impressions of Black Churches', *West Africa*, 4 Apr. 1988, 596–7.

Uncollected Poems

'I came on stage', *West Africa*, 29 July 1980, 1391.
'For Julie', *West Africa*, 9 Nov. 1981, 2654.
'Newton Enigmas', *The Times* (Saturday Review), 4 July 1992, 41.
'A Song for Rwanda', *Independent*, 1 Oct. 1994.
'Soul of the Nation', *Guardian*, 20 July 1999, 2.

Radio and Television Appearances

'London to Arcadia', *Great Railway Journeys*, producer Jonathon Stedall, executive producer David Taylor, BBC2, Wednesday, 6 Oct. 1996, 9.30 p.m.

The Brains Trust, with the art historian Ludmilla Jordanova, theologian Canon Tom Wright, and Merton Professor of English at Oxford, John Carey; chaired by Joan Bakewell, BBC Radio 3, Saturday, 2 Sept. 2000, 10.15p.m.

WORKS ON BEN OKRI

Selected Interviews

Ross, Jean W. Ross (taped interview, 6 June 1971), 'CA Interview', in Donna Olendorf (ed.), *Contemporary Authors: A Bio-Bibliographic Guide to Current Authors in Fiction, General Nonfiction, Poetry, Journalism, Drama, Motion Pictures, Television and Other Fields*, 138 (Detroit: Gale Research, 1993), 337–41.

Shakespeare, Nicholas, 'Fantasies Born in the Ghetto', *The Times*, 24 July 1986, 23.

Philip, Howard, 'There Is Wonder Here', *The Times*, 24 Oct. 1991, 15.

Wilkinson, Jane (Italian-based literary scholar), 'Interview with Ben Okri', *Guardian*, 24 Oct. 1991, 23.

Muir, Philip, 'An Author in Search of Humility', *The Times*, 25 Oct. 1991, 15.

Grant, Linda (novelist and later Orange Prize Winner), 'The Lonely Road from Twilight to Hard Sun', *Observer*, 27 Oct. 1991.

Ryan, Alan (New York journalist), 'Talking with Ben Okri', *Newsday*, 19 July 1992.

Green, Jonathon, 'Ben Okri Reflects on a Year as the Miss World of Bookdom', *The Times*, 13 Oct. 1992, 14.

Newton, Carolyn, 'An Interview with Ben Okri', *South African Literary Review*, 2/3 (1992), 5–6.

Hunter, Davies, 'Ben Okri's Green-Apple, Left-Handed Sort of a Day', *Independent*, 23 Mar. 1993, 18.

Wilde, Jonathon, 'A Very English Story', *New Yorker*, 6 Mar. 1996, 96–106.

Hattersley, Roy (former Labour Deputy Leader), 'Ben Okri: A Man in Two Minds', The Guardian Profile, *Guardian*, 21 Aug. 1999, 6.

Criticism

Appiah, Anthony, 'Spiritual Realism' (review of *The Famished Road*), in *Nation*, 3 Aug. 1992, 146–8.

Appiah, Anthony, review of *Songs of Enchantment*, in *Washington Post* (*Book World*), 3 Oct. 1993 (late edn), 5.

Bardolph, Jacqueline, 'Azaro, Saleem and Askar: Brothers in Allegory', *Commonwealth Essays and Studies*, 15/1 (1992), 45–51.

Boehmer, Elleke, review of *The Famished Road*, in *Novel*, 26 (1993), 268.

—— 'The Matter as Metaphor in Contemporary African Literature', *English Studies in Transition* (1993), 320–31.

Bryce, Jane, 'Out of Earth' (review of *Flowers and Shadows*), in *The Times Literary Supplement*, 19 Sept. 1980, 1047.

Chaudhuri, Amit, 'A Love Story with Compound Interest' (review of *Dangerous Love*), in *Spectator*, 20 Apr. 1996, 42–3.

Cribb, Timothy, 'Transformations in the Fiction of Ben Okri', *English Studies in Transition* (1993), 445–50.

Dandy, Jo, 'Magic and Realism in Ben Okri's *The Famished Road*, *Songs of Enchantment* and *Astonishing the Gods*: An Examination of Conflicting Cultural Influences and Narrative Traditions', in *Kiss and Quarrel: Yoruba/English, Strategies of Mediation* (Birmingham University African Studies Series No. 5; Birmingham: Centre of West African Studies, 2000), 45–63.

Fraser, Robert, 'Meticulous Acid' (review of *Incidents at the Shrine*), in *West Africa*, 3598, 18 Aug. 1986, 1738.

—— 'Incantatory Beauty' (review of *Stars of the New Curfew*), in *Third World Quarterly*, 11/2 (Apr. 1989), 181–3.

—— 'Carrion Comfort and Magical Strains' (review of *The Famished Road*), in *Independent* (Weekend Books), 1 June 1991, 28.

—— 'Ben Okri at Trinity', *CAM* (*The Cambridge Alumni Magazine*) (published on behalf of The Cambridge Foundation) (Spring 1992), 35.

—— 'The Magic of the Jackals' (review of *Songs of Enchantment*), in *West Africa*, 3942, 12–18 Apr. 1993, 616.

—— 'The Shield of Art' (review of *Dangerous Love*), in *West Africa*, 4108, 15–21 July 1996, 1122.

—— 'Killing the Minotaur' (review of *Birds of Heaven* and *A Way of Being Free*), in *West Africa*, 4146, 21–27 Apr. 1997, 653.

—— 'Kariba's Fall', in Flora Veit-Wild and Anthony Chennells (eds), *Emerging Perspectives on Dambudzo Marechera* (Trenton, NJ: Africa World Press, 1998), 105–18. Contains a cameo appearance of Okri as a young man.

—— review of Ato Quayson, *Strategic Transformations in Nigerian Writing*, and Ben Okri, *Infinite Riches*, in *Wasafiri*, 29 (Spring 1999), 86–7.

Gates, Henry Louis, Jr, 'Between the Living and the Unborn' (review of *The Famished Road*), *New York Times* (*Book Review*), 28 June 1992 (late edn), sect. 7.3.

Hawley, J. C, 'Ben Okri's Spirit Child: Abiku, Migration and Post-modernity', *Research in African Literatures*, 26/1 (Spring 1995), 30–9.

Lasdun, James, 'Sunlight and Chaos' (review of Ben Okri, *Flowers and Shadows*, and Dambudzo Marechera, *Black Sunlight*), in *New Statesman*, 19 Dec. 1980, 45.

Niven, Alastair, 'Achebe and Okri: Contrasts in the Response to the Civil War', in Jacqueline Bardolph (ed.), *Short Fiction in New Literatures in English: Proceedings of the Nice Conference of the European Association for Commonwealth Literature and Language Studies* (Nice: Faculté des Lettres et Sciences Humaines, 1989), 277–83.

Ogunsanwo, O., 'Intertextuality and Post-Colonial Literature in Ben Okri's *Famished Road*', *Research in African Literatures*, 26/1 (1995), 40–52.

Omotoso, Kole, 'Fantastic Dreams of the Poor' (review of *Songs of Enchantment*), in *Manchester Guardian Weekly*, 11 Apr. 1993, 28.

Porlock, Harvey, 'On the Critical List', *Sunday Times*, 14 July 1991, section 6 (Books), 6.

Quayson, Ato, 'Esoteric Webwork as Nervous System: Reading the Fantastic in Ben Okri's Writing', in Abdulrazak Gurnah (ed.), *Essays on African Writing II* (1995), 144–58.

—— 'Textuality: Tutuola, Okri and the Relationship of Literary Practice to Oral Traditions', in Stewart Brown (ed.), *The Pressures of the Text: Orality, Texts and the Telling of Tales* (Birmingham University African Studies Series No. 4; University of Birmingham: Centre of West African Studies, 1995), 96–117.

—— *Strategic Transformations in Nigerian Writing: Rev. Samuel Johnson, Amos Tutuola, Wole Soyinka, Ben Okri* (Oxford: James Currey, 1997), especially chapters 6 and 7, and the appendix.

Richards, David, 'A History of Interpretations: Dislocated Mimesis in the Writings of Neil Bissoondath and Ben Okri', *English Studies in Transition* (1993), 74–82.

Thorpe, Michael, 'Fictions of Freedom: Recent Commonwealth Writing', *Encounter*, 68 (1987), 42–6.

Wilkinson, Jane, *Talking with African Writers* (London: James Currey, 1992).

Wright, Derek, review of *Songs of Enchantment*, in *International Fiction Review*, 22 (1995), 111.

—— 'Whither Nigerian Fiction? Into the Nineties', *Journal of Modern African Studies*, 33 (1995), 315–32.

OTHER RELEVANT WORKS

Chinua Achebe, *Girls at War* (London: Heinemann Educational Books, 1972).

Erivwo, Samuel U., *The Urhobo, the Isoko and the Itsekiri* (Ibadan: Daystar Press, 1979).

Ikime, Obaro, *Niger Delta Rivalry: Itsekiri–Urhobo Relations and the European Presence, 1884–1936* (London: Longman, 1977).

—— *The Member for Warri Province: The Life and Times of Chief Mukoro Moroe of Warri, 1890–1948* (Ibadan: Institute of African Studies, 1977).

Iyayi, Festus, *Violence* (London: Longman, 1979).

—— *Heroes* (London: Longman, 1986).

Maja-Pierce, Adewale, *Loyalties* (London: Longman, 1986).

Okpewho, Isidore, *The Last Duty* (London: Longman, 1976).

Saro-Wiwa, Ken, *On a Darkling Plain* (Port Harcourt: Saros Publishers, 1989).

—— *A Month and a Day: A Detention Diary* (London: Penguin, 1995).

Index